LANDSCAPE
PHOTOGRAPHER OF THE YEAR
COLLECTION 02

Senior Art Editor: Nick Otway
Managing Editor: Paul Mitchell
Image retouching and colour repro: Mike Moody
Production: Lyn Kirby
Indexer: Hilary Bird

Produced by AA Publishing
© Automobile Association Developments Limited 2008

Published by AA Publishing (a trading name of Automobile Association
Developments Limited, whose registered office is Fanum House, Basing View,
Basingstoke RG21 4EA; registered number 1878835).

A3935

ISBN: 978-0-7495-5905-2

A CIP catalogue record for this book is available from the British Library.

The contents of this book are believed correct at the time of printing. Nevertheless,
the publishers cannot be held responsible for any errors or omissions or for
changes in the details given in this book or for the consequences of any reliance on
the information provided by the same. This does not affect your statutory rights.

Origination by Keene Group, Andover
Printed and bound in Italy by Printer Trento S.r.l.

www.theAA.com/travel

MARK BAUER ···⦂

A frosty dawn, Eyebridge, River Stour, Dorset, England

I had headed to the River Stour near Wimborne, hoping for a wintry dawn shot of the river.
Having failed to find a composition on the riverbank, I was drawn to the strong lines of the
bridge. A wide-angle lens enabled me to enhance the perspective of the converging lines.

CONTENTS

MICHAEL DUDLEY ···⟩

Eynsford, Kent, England

Taken early one spring morning while trying a new lens. Eynsford is on the A225 between Dartford and Sevenoaks.

INTRODUCTION

THE COMPETITION

Take a view, the Landscape Photographer of the Year Award, is the idea of Charlie Waite, one of today's most respected landscape photographers. After the high standard of the first year, this second collection proves that the Awards are the perfect platform to showcase the very best photography of the British landscape. Support from all the major leading tourist agencies of the UK has been invaluable and entries were received from all corners of the nation.

Open to images of the United Kingdom, Isle of Man and the Channel Islands, Take a view is divided into two main sections, the Landscape Photographer of the Year Award and the Young Landscape Photographer of the Year Award. With a total prize fund exceeding £20,000 and an exhibition of winning and commended entries at London's National Theatre, Take a view has become a desirable annual competition for photographers of all ages.

All images within this book were judged by the panel as Commended or above, a high accolade given the total entry.

www.landscapephotographeroftheyear.co.uk
www.take-a-view.co.uk

KEY SUPPORTERS

THE CATEGORIES

Classic View

For images that capture the beauty and variety of the UK landscape. The rugged cliffs and endless beaches of the coastline, the majestic mountains of the highlands and the verdant splendour of the National Parks. Recognisable and memorable – these are true classics.

Living the View

Featuring images of people interacting with the outdoors – working or playing in the UK landscape. From the peaceful tranquillity of an early morning fishing trip to a walk in an urban park or the thrills of kite surfing, these images illustrate the many ways in which we connect with our outdoor environment.

Your View

What does the UK landscape mean to you? Sometimes intensely personal and often very conceptual, the parameters of this category are far-reaching, with images showing a whole range of emotions and perspectives. Subjects vary from the peace of a misty Scottish loch to the tumultuous and damaging waves of a storm on the Yorkshire coast.

Phone View

The key to this category is spontaneity. There may be no tripods or long lenses, but the great advantage of the camera phone is that it is always with you, so there are plenty of chances to capture the unexpected.

SPECIAL PRIZES

The Visit Wales Award

For the best image of Wales entered into the Adult 'Living the View' category.

The Enjoy England Award

For the best urban image of England entered into any Adult category.

The Páramo Mountain Award

For the best mountain image entered into any Adult category.

The Lowepro Environment Award

For the best Youth and best Adult image reflecting the beauty of our precious natural environment.

WITH THANKS TO

FOREWORD
BY CHARLIE WAITE

LANDSCAPE PHOTOGRAPHER OF THE YEAR 2008

The aim of this Award is to bring the joys of making a landscape photograph to as many people as possible and to promote both landscape photography and the United Kingdom. Landscape Photographer of the Year 2007 gave us the best start I could have imagined and this year shows that we are, indeed, a nation with our landscape in our hearts.

Perhaps to be truly successful, a landscape image should, at best, evoke an emotion in the viewer or, at least, certainly stimulate a response of some kind. A technically superb image can still be strangely devoid of emotion and it is the photographers' wish to try to convey at least an element of the emotions that they themselves felt at the time of making.

An image can give rise to a whole gamut of emotions; from a feeling of being very small and insignificant against the might of the sea to the feeling of tranquillity and peace from a pastoral valley.

In recent years, photography has become increasingly popular as a medium and I applaud this. In an ideal world, I would love everyone to have the chance to experience positive emotions from an interaction with their environment via one of the most remarkable of creative tools; the camera. But while the camera is bursting with potential, it is nevertheless a tool essentially to look 'through'.

The recognition that an image exists to be made in the first place is just as important to the success of the image as the location and the light.

Recently, I was fortunate enough to be asked to write and illustrate an article for a book on the 'Icons of England' for the Council of Protection for Rural England. I chose the wartime airfields of Lincolnshire as my subject, partly because of a direct family connection. I enjoyed the whole experience more than I could have imagined and I like to think that the emotion I felt at the time of making the photograph shows in the resulting image – although that will be down to the viewer to decide.

Giving ourselves a theme to work to can really help focus our photography. Taking a series of images that makes us feel happy by evoking memories of childhood, or that makes us uneasy and out of our natural element can focus minds and so make the viewer of the image feel more intensely about your picture.

The success of our first exhibition at London's National Theatre really brought home an obvious, but often overlooked, point to me. The Landscape Photographer of the Year Award does not only appeal to those who want to make beautiful and interesting images but also to those who want to look at them. Although these groups overlap, there are people that are unique to one group or the other and the total numbers are vast – and that helps to explains the 'spreading ripples' that are making the Awards such a worthwhile venture with which all can be involved.

I strongly believe that our surroundings and our appreciation of them can have a direct effect on our sense of well-being. Towards the end of his career, the artist Peter Paul Rubens, after many years of painting dramatic religious scenes and portraits, allowed more time for personal work, including a number of bucolic landscapes of the area surrounding his home. Interaction with the landscape gives us a bit of time out; perhaps a chance to reflect on and contemplate the great fundamentals of human existence. I would strenuously argue that the camera is a most wonderful medium with which we can engage in this interaction and emerge the richer for it.

When seeking a location for a landscape image, there is a tendency to gravitate towards the recognised and beautiful photographic views – Durdle Door, Glencoe and Dunstanburgh Castle to name but a few. This is no surprise – their photographic merit and worthiness is unquestionable. But one of the key strengths of our islands is their variety and it is just as possible to make a memorable, graphic image from a wall and field pattern just down the road or an urban viaduct cutting through a local park. I certainly agree with judge Damien Demolder, when he says that it is often the subtle images that can be the most enduring.

William Blake saw England as a 'green and pleasant land'. I will use a bit of artistic licence here and extend this to the whole of the UK. We are also known as an 'island race' and seem pleased with this label that can be seen to give us an identity as a nation. Over the past two years of Take a view, the idea that we are an island has dominated. The images of seascapes have outnumbered those of rolling downs, moors and dales by at least three to one. Crashing waves undoubtedly bring drama and we have always loved the changing moods of the sea, but who knows what next year will bring? And that's the beauty of the Awards. All images are judged on visual merit – locations are not known, which reveals some interesting results. This year was a good one for bridges – structures that span water and so are striking examples of man's attempts to tame nature. The overall winner is chosen from any one of the adult categories and so will not always be a 'classic' landscape. This year's winner is a prime example of an image that successfully evoked an emotion that beat all opposition.

Just for a minute, I would like to touch on the technical side of the images. We aim to encourage creativity and so have allowed entrants to digitally manipulate entries. However, there is a strict proviso – the integrity of the landscape must be retained at all times. Humans have adjusted the way they present themselves and their world through art for centuries. Holbein risked losing his head when he painted too flattering a representation of Anne of Cleves to 'sell' her to a demanding King. Subtlety is always required – over-manipulation ruins images, with the viewer perhaps distrusting the image as a result. It was refreshing to see that, for those entries that were adjusted, it was generally done with a sleight of hand that enhanced rather than destroyed.

I was really thrilled that the UK's leading tourist agencies came together to support the Awards. It is such a perfect match for us and the fact that all the main regions are involved ensured a positive response from entrants in all corners of the nation. Although locations are not used for judging, the final results have proved that there is certainly beauty and interest to be had wherever you travel. Again, this year, our judging panel gave generously of their time and enthusiasm and we were definitely spoilt for choice. I find it intriguing that, despite all having worked within the creative sphere for many years, one judge may dislike an image that another loves most dearly. But that's what makes us human and makes our emotional response to the landscape different to that of the person standing two feet away.

Over the years, our wonderful realm has been perceived in various ways – politically, artistically, proudly and, sometimes, disparagingly. Despite all the bad news that infiltrates our lives today, our love for our country is key. There are many things that could be improved – there always will be and we are constantly being told of them. But the landscape and its enduring quality is symbolic of a nation of which there is, and will always be, much to be proud.

What will next year bring? – I can't wait to find out.

THE JUDGES

Valerie Singleton

Presenter and travel writer

A small-screen legend, Valerie is still most recognised as one of the best-loved *Blue Peter* presenters but has since worked on many landmark programmes including *Nationwide*, *PM* and *The Money Programme*. She was awarded an OBE in 1994 for her servies to broadcasting. Valerie is a regular travel writer for a number of national publications and stories from her life were recently featured in the *Daily Mail*.

After living in London for many years, Valerie is now based in one of England's most beautiful counties, Dorset, and loves exploring the coastal scenery and beautiful houses of the area.

Charlie Waite

Landscape Photographer

Charlie Waite is firmly established as one of the world's most celebrated landscape photographers. He has published 28 books on photography and has held over 30 solo exhibitions across Europe, the USA, Japan and Australia, including three very successful exhibitions in the gallery at the OXO Tower in London, each visited by over 12,000 visitors.

His company, Light & Land, runs photographic tours, courses and workshops worldwide that are dedicated to inspiring photographers and improving their photography. This is achieved with the help of a select team of specialist photographic leaders.

He is the man behind the Landscape Photographer of the Year Awards and this ties in perfectly with his desire to share his passion and appreciation of the beauty of our world.

Damien Demolder

Amateur Photographer magazine Editor

Damien is the editor of *Amateur Photographer* magazine, the world's oldest weekly magazine for photography enthusiasts, and a very keen photographer too. He started his photographic professional life at the age of 18, but since taking up the editorship of the magazine he has been able to return to his amateur status – shooting what he likes, for his own pleasure.

With interests in all areas of photography, Damien does not have a favourite subject, only subjects he is currently concentrating on. At the moment his efforts are going into landscapes and social documentary. When judging photography competitions Damien looks for signs of genuine talent or hard work. Originality is important, as is demonstrating a real understanding of the subject and an ability to capture it in a realistic manner. He says 'Drama is always eye-catching, but often it is the subtle, calm and intelligent images that are more pleasing and enduring'.

Jasmine Teer

Britain on View Manager/Art Director

Jasmine's passion for photography began at a very young age and after training in large-format photography and working as a photographic technician at Portsmouth Art College, she graduated from London College of Printing in 1999.

Since 2005, Jasmine has managed the online image library, Britain on View, which is owned by VisitBritain and she has managed and art directed over 300 shoots around the UK. Jasmine's love for photography has also led her to curate the photographic exhibition, Britain on View, for the past three years in London that has featured work from some of the UK's best landscape photographers, including Charlie Waite and the winner of the first Landscape Photographer of the Year Award, Jon Gibbs.

Tracy Hallett

Outdoor Photography magazine Editor

Tracy Hallett is editor of *Outdoor Photography* magazine. She has co-authored three photography books, and her work has been featured in 20 consumer magazines, as well as on the walls of The Photographers' Gallery and The National Portrait Gallery in London.

Tracy is a practising photographer, with a special interest in macro work. Her latest project involves photographing all of the wild flower species in Sussex, but she also enjoys shooting the broader landscapes around the coastline of the UK. She is a regular contributor to the stock library, Alamy.

John Langley

National Theatre Manager

John is the Theatre Manager of the National Theatre, on London's South Bank. Alongside its three stages, summer outdoor events programme and early evening platform performances, the National has become renowned for its full and varied free exhibitions programme. Held regularly in two bespoke spaces, these exhibitions are an important, ongoing part of London's art and photographic scene. John is responsible for these shows and has organised over 300 exhibitions and played a significant role in presenting innovative and exciting photography to a wide and discerning audience.

When escaping from the urban bustle of the capital, John particularly loves the coastal scenery of the United Kingdom, with the north Norfolk coast and Purbeck in Dorset being particular favourites.

Monica Allende

Sunday Times Magazine Picture Editor

Monica started her career in publishing; commissioning travel photography where sourcing idyllic landscapes was the objective. For the last seven years, she has been Picture Editor for *The Sunday Times Magazine*.

Although she works with images every day of her life, Monica still gets excited about the variety and creativity of photography and champions up-and-coming photographers. She is interested in the increasing accessibility of photography and the changing attitudes of young people towards the art.

She likes extreme landscapes; raw nature that gives a feeling of infinity and appears unchanged by the human hand. Her favourite element is water and so the coastal landscape, particularly of North Devon and Cornwall, has provided unforgettable visual images, but as an urbanite, born and bred among concrete, the urban landscape speaks to her in a familiar language.

Nick White

Epson UK

Nick's photographic life began with his father's aerial photography company. From a school holiday job in the black and white darkroom, he later joined full-time and was involved in both commercial and aerial photography while running the in-house processing facility.

It was natural that an appreciation of aerial landscapes developed and he feels that this was the origin of his interest in landscape photography today.

Nick's career switched to the trade side of photography, with lengthy stints at Durst and Fujifilm, before he joined the Epson large-format team three years ago.

A keen sailor for many years, Nick is based on England's South Coast, and this is an area he is always happy to come home to.

Pre-Judging Panel

The pre-judging panel has had the difficult task of selecting the best images to go through to the final shortlist. Every image entered into the competition was meticulously analysed before the final list was put through to face the final team of judges.

Sarah Fransden, Britain on View

Born into the family of a passionate antiquarian print seller, Sarah has always been surrounded by the power of the image and her entire professional career has been based in the stock photography industry. Originally at the Image Bank, she then worked for seven years at the National Trust Photo Library, where she began her deep admiration for some of the country's leading landscape photographers including Joe Cornish and David Noton. In 2005, Sarah was able to widen her knowledge by moving to Britain on View, the online image library of VisitBritain, as the Image Editor. Working with a wider range of British-based photographers, Sarah feels lucky to work with some of the best landscape photography from around the British Isles every day. She appreciates all kinds of photographic styles and loves the rich and diverse nature of the landscape in Great Britain. She is drawn to so many of its stunning areas – from the wilds of the Scottish Highlands, through to the drama of the Peak District and the Brecon Beacons, down to the beauty of Cornwall's coastline to name but a few.

Trevor Parr, Parr-Joyce Partnership

Trevor's lifelong love of photography started at Art College. He became an assistant to a number of fashion photographers before setting up on his own in a Covent Garden studio. He moved to the Stock/Agency business, seeking new photography and acting as art director on a number of shoots. In the late 1980s, he started the Parr-Joyce Partnership with Christopher Joyce and this agency marketed conceptual, landscape and fine art photography to poster, card and calendar companies. Trevor also owned a specialist landscape library that was later sold to a larger agency. He now concentrates on running Parr-Joyce from his base in the south of England.

Martin Halfhide and Robin Bernard, Bayeux

Robin and Martin are co-owners and directors of Bayeux, a professional imaging company that opened in 2001 and is now the largest in London's West End. With an extensive background in the pro-lab industry, both have experience in many technical areas. They were at London-based Ceta in the 1980s and then went on to be responsible for photographer liaison at Tapestry during the 1990s. Although very much attached to a London lifestyle, Robin escapes to the country at regular intervals, particularly the English Lakes. He likes both powerful, dramatic landscape images and minimal understated images – but is less enthusiastic about those in between. He dislikes 'copy-cat' images that are imitations of original styles. Martin favours the wilds of Scotland and visits every year.

and Charlie Waite

AWARDS ORGANISER: Diana Leppard

I owe a huge debt of gratitude to Diana Leppard. Take a view: The Landscape Photographer of the Year Award would not have been possible without her total dedication, enthusiasm and just plain hard work.

Charlie Waite

MIKE CURRY ···⟩

Greenwich Park, London, England

Greenwich Park has been much photographed over the years and I wanted to create a unique image. The addition of the new 'Greenwich Eye' to the skyline and the arrival of my converted Olympus E1 gave me the incentive to try and create something new. I wanted to show the contrast between the new and old buildings, and I liked the way infra-red brought out the detail of the foliage on the trees. I waited for a good spread of people in the frame and took the photo!

LANDSCAPE
PHOTOGRAPHER OF THE YEAR

LANDSCAPE PHOTOGRAPHER OF THE YEAR 2008

OVERALL WINNER

⋯ **GARY EASTWOOD**

Barney on a jetty in December, Hove beach, East Sussex, England

This shot was taken at 4.30pm on a stormy December afternoon. I was walking along the beach with my dog Barney in unpromising grey and windy conditions, when the sun broke through the clouds and bathed everything in a glorious amber light. I quickly tried to capture the jetty and some nearby windsurfers (one of which can be seen in the distance), but Barney kept wandering into the frame and standing in that particular spot! It's now one of my favourite images as it encapsulates the best aspects of living by the sea in winter.

Judge's choice Valerie Singleton

YOUNG LANDSCAPE PHOTOGRAPHER OF THE YEAR 2008

OVERALL WINNER

GABRIELLE BARNES ···⇢

Poppies and maize at sunset, Hadley Down, Dorset, England

I had been looking for a great composition for my school art project and on this particular evening was out with my Dad who was taking pictures. I chose to stop in a field slightly off the path I normally take and saw this field that had been cut, all except for one long strip made up of poppies, maize and some wild flowers. The light was really lovely and I was lucky enough to capture this moment.

Lowepro Award for BEST ENVIRONMENTAL image (Youth)

CLASSIC VIEW
adult class

CLASSIC VIEW ADULT CLASS WINNER

⁛⋯ SIMON BUTTERWORTH

'Diamonds aren't forever', Loch Dochard, Scotland

I kept to my golden rule of wearing wellies when photographing near water, but the level was within millimetres of my boot tops while capturing this image. Every time I moved I felt the trickle of freezing cold water run down to my thick, woolly socks. I had a very cold and squelchy 90-minute walk back to my car as the cold winter night settled over the glen.

Páramo Award winner for BEST MOUNTAIN picture

CLASSIC VIEW ADULT CLASS RUNNER-UP

GARY WAIDSON ···⯈

Yule morn, Tandlewood, Lancashire, England

I had spotted the potential of this location quite some time before
but the conditions had never been right when I had been around.
Taking our dog, Skadi, out for a walk on the morning of Yule, I
noticed a heavy fog had risen up overnight. I grabbed the camera
and we headed, full of hope, straight for this spot. The dense mist
drifting between the mature beech trees wreathed the wood with a
sense of mystery and magic perfectly in keeping with the day.

GRAHAM HOBBS

GRAHAM HOBBS   HIGHLY COMMENDED

Kingston Lacy Beech Avenue at dawn, Dorset, England

This is an important year for the avenue of beech trees that runs for a mile or so along the B3082 Blandford Road towards Kingston Lacy. The National Trust, the body responsible for the avenue, is aware that the two-hundred-year-old trees are reaching the end of their natural lives and will increasingly need to be felled for the safety of passing traffic. Before the integrity of the avenue is lost by too many gaps appearing, they are encouraging photographers to record this glorious local feature in its different moods throughout the seasons. The fresh greens of springtime seemed to me to demand the first light of dawn – a time with the added bonus of there being no traffic to spoil the timelessness of the image.

27

<... **PAUL HOLLOWAY**   HIGHLY COMMENDED

Trotternish from the Quiraing, Skye, Scotland

I camped out here to be in good time for sunrise. Before turning
in for the night I scouted around for viewpoints. Down a little gully
I found this gnarled old tree clinging onto the hillside. There was
something about it I found quite moving. Despite its precarious
position it was stubbornly growing upward, thrusting its branches
towards the sky. Life will not be denied! The next morning I opened
the tent to find a grey world with no sign of a sunrise. After a couple
of hours the cloud began to break up with the light flooding through
bringing the landscape to life. Well worth waiting for.

MARK BAUER ···>   HIGHLY COMMENDED

First frost, Sturminster Newton, Dorset, England

Sturminster Newton Mill is normally photographed in summer, lit
by the early morning sun. Here it is shown photographed in the first
heavy frost of the winter. By taking a low viewpoint, I was able to
use the frost-covered teasels as a natural frame for this view of
the mill.

FAN FU ⟶

[HIGHLY COMMENDED]

Storm brewing at Tynemouth, England

After travelling up to Tynemouth, with the hope of fine weather to photograph the lighthouse, I approached to see this amazing cloud formation. In a light rain and a very strong wind that saw me leaning against a lamp post to try and maintain my balance, I was very fortunate to be able to capture the drama of the clouds over the sea before they quickly dissipated. Truly, one of those rare moments of being in the right place at the right time.

The lighthouse at Spurn Point, Yorkshire

The lighthouse is situated on the north bank of the entrance to the River Humber, near the end of the narrow sand spit of Spurn at Spurn Point. Now just an empty shell, the lighthouse has not been used since it was closed down in October 1986. As the sun began to lower one February evening, I noticed the light striking the lighthouse and the weather-beaten groynes. My aim was to capture the groynes and colourful pebbles strewn across the beach, to add depth to the scene with the lighthouse as the focal point.

Judge's choice John Langley

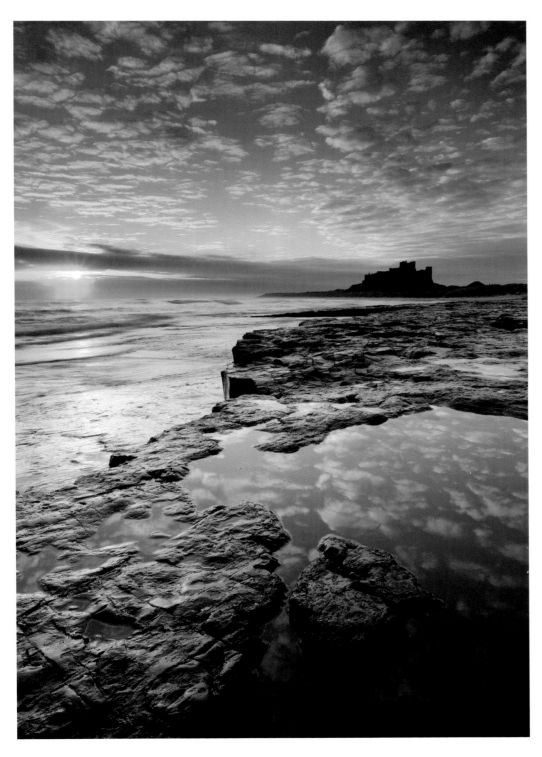

⋯ ADAM BURTON   HIGHLY COMMENDED

Autumn sunrise at Bamburgh Castle, Northumberland, England

My first photographic trip to Northumberland was in fact a getaway with my wife to celebrate our first wedding anniversary. I brought the camera, hoping to capture one or two locations along the way. Unfortunately, the weather wasn't going to play along; on the first evening I attempted pretty unsuccessfully to photograph the coast in gale force conditions. Feeling inspired by the fantastic coastline, and determined not to be put off by the weather I returned for sunrise the next morning, only to encounter more of the same.

I grew more resolute as the days wore on, being out every single sunrise and sunset, ready for a glimpse of the sun that was not prepared to show itself. On the final day I was again in position when the clouds gradually dispersed and the sun rose over the horizon. It was a spectacular sight and well worth all the effort involved. Luckily for me my wife was in agreement!

GIOVANNI RUSSELLO

Storm over Pen yr Ole Wen, Snowdonia National Park, Wales

I arrived at Llyn Idwal when it was still dark. The sky was crossed with threatening clouds coming in from the sea. I decided to set up my gear on a stretch of the Idwal River, just beside a bridge that crosses it. I composed the picture using the river as a leading path and focused on Pen yr Ole Wen, standing tall and proud as the guardian of the Carneddau plateau. To do this, I had to set the tripod near the water surface, so I had my boots in the freezing water as well! On the way back, I realised that I was not the only photographer out there and decided to get closer to say hello. What a surprise when I discovered that my fellow photographer was Steve Lewis from Light & Land. We talked about 'Take a view' and he suggested that I enter the 2008 competition. So, here it is, the one that I took that day!

IAN CAMERON

The Three Sisters of Glencoe, Scotland

The A82 meanders down the Glencoe valley squeezed between the magnificent peaks of the Three Sisters and the Aonach Eagach ridge, one of the scariest mountain hikes in the UK. During the transition weeks between spring and summer, the grass-covered slopes are rich and luxuriant, particularly after rain soaks them through. A brief summer storm had swept through the valley and I waited until the rain had slowed to a light drizzle, then climbed up the slope on the opposite side of the A82 finding a stony plateau below which I could hide the road. The storm cleared as quickly as it came and I saw a finger of sunlight break through the clouds and watched transfixed as it spread up the verdant slopes along the valley. I waited until the last possible moment before direct sunlight hit me, and took the shot.

VERENA POPP-HACKNER

Boulders in surf at Rackwick Bay, Orkney Islands, Scotland

It is pretty impossible (I think) not to be attracted to and impressed by these boulders, which are strewn all around Rackwick Bay. Since rain, along with cloudy skies, was the usual weather during my stay here, I focused on more detailed or intimate landscape shots. I lost myself for hours in framing images and looking for compositions as tides were rising and falling. I stumbled upon this group of boulders a couple of times, but felt that it would be the best time to expose some sheets of film only when the tide was high enough for the waves to wash over the most colourful rocks. Still, I could not be sure about the final outcome until I was back at home, weeks later. One of the (few) things I envy about digital shooters is being able to see the desired effects right away on the monitor...

MIKE SHARPLES

Laig Bay, Isle of Eigg, Scotland

This image was captured in the mid-morning in the spring of 2008. The Isle of Eigg and, particularly, Laig Bay, is a fascinating place – the weather can change in a moment from bright sunshine to lashing rain. There being no public transport on the Island, the 90-minute walk from the Ferry Port to Laig Bay with photo kit is quite a trip, but once you arrive that is soon forgotten. Taking landscape images is one of my passions – I have always been fascinated by natural light, particularly in Scotland and the Western Isles. I regard the quality and direction of light as the most important elements in a landscape. Many of my images are captured in those golden hours; just before dusk and after dawn.

DUNCAN McMILLAN ⋯⋗

The Humber Bridge at night, East Yorkshire, England

The stars were concealed from the naked eye by a light mist on this chilly December evening on the Humber Estuary. The long exposure allowed them to burn through, revealing myriad constellations in the southern sky. Orion, the Hunter, can be seen clearly in the centre, with Canis Major (the Great Dog, the larger of Orion's two hunting dogs) at his feet, chasing Lepus, the Hare. Also visible is Taurus, the Bull and Eridanus, the River.

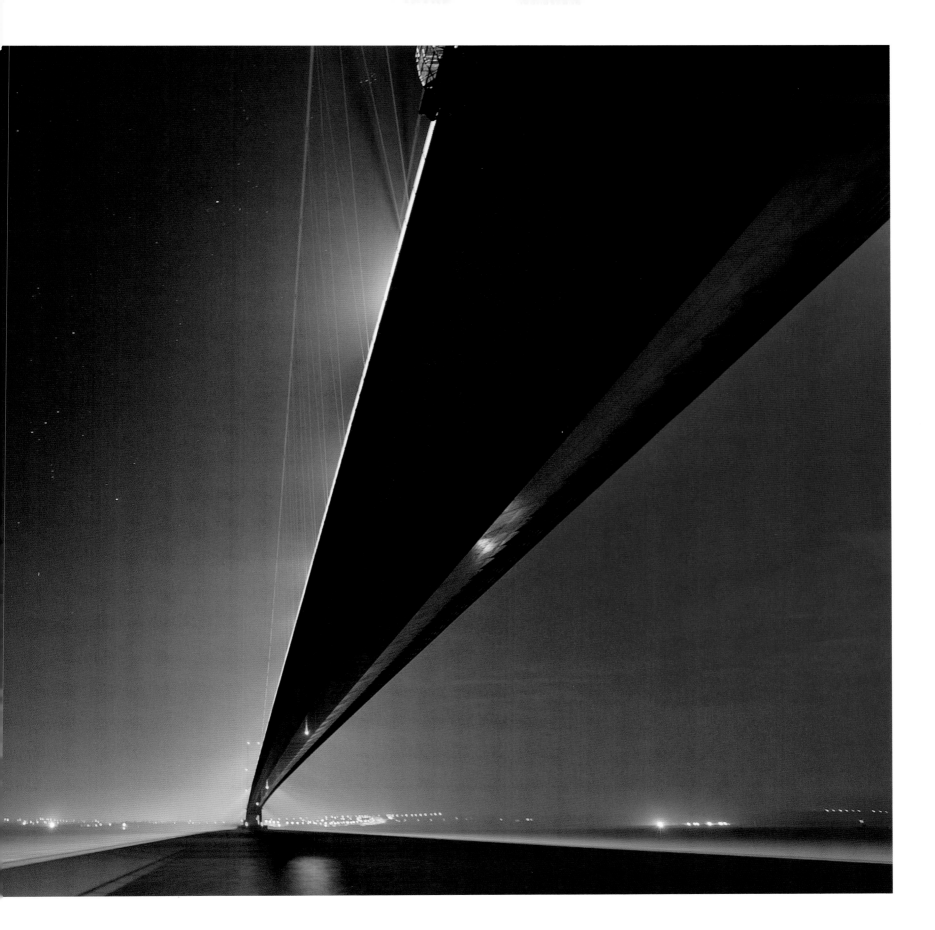

STEVE GRAY

'Stillness', Lake of Menteith, The Trossachs, Scotland

On the first afternoon of a trip to The Trossachs in mid-April, we visited the shoreline of the Lake of Menteith. It was a time in the afternoon when prolonged showers had finally moved away, leaving exceptionally calm conditions, with mist and moisture still hanging in the air. Working along the shore, I captured a series of images concentrating on abstract and minimalist compositions that seemed to suit the mood of the day. They turned out to be my favourite images from the trip – I think they convey something of the calm, almost eerie atmosphere of that afternoon.

Judge's choice Monica Allende

DAVID CLAPP

Wistman's Wood, Dartmoor, Devon

Wistman's Wood is a snapshot of Dartmoor in times past. This high altitude valley is filled with stunted oak trees and remains a wonderful reference of how the moors used to be. A haunted woodland? Perhaps. It is shrouded in superstition with tales of druids, hellhounds, snakes and the living dead. Only fog can compliment this treachery and the conditions one spring Friday were perfect, or so I thought. After the forest appeared in the mist, I set up at a favourite place only to watch the thick blanket of cloud remain above the canopy. An hour later and still nothing, my patience was wearing thin. Then the fog began to descend in five-minute bursts, filling the scene with the magic I had pre-visualised two years before. Filled with mysterious light, it was easy to see how these legends and stories remain close to our hearts today.

41

⚜ RICHARD OSBOURNE

The Cuillin Hills, Isle of Skye, Scotland

I don't remember seeing a more hypnotically beautiful sight than this one. I'd driven across the Skye Bridge one September evening and the Cuillin Hills had been drawing my eyes with their magnetic combination of light, cloud formations and sea. This spectacular scene appeared in the rear-view mirror as I left Skye for the mainland. I had to stop. I spent an hour photographing it until the light faded. The monochrome treatment conveyed the drama of the scene most acutely, with the tiny house showing the grand scale.

✧ PETER RIBBECK

'Morning glow', West Kilbride, Scotland

This shot was taken at the back of the village of West Kilbride. It was an early start and a long hike, but well worth the effort. As I got to the top of the hill, I could see the mist starting to roll off the neighbouring peak. I got the shots I wanted and started my descent; by this time the mist was on top of me and was giving a nice warm diffused light. I walked past an old abandoned farmhouse with this interesting tree next to it. The mist began to lift momentarily and the sun began to shine through, giving a lovely glow behind the tree. I managed to take two quick shots before the mist closed in once more. I felt very lucky to have been in the right place at just the right time!

🔱 GAIL JOHNSON

Rough at Roker, Sunderland, England

I had to hide behind a wall in order to take this photo as the wind was so strong it was blowing the tripod over. This event only happened once in the hours I was there and I just roared with laughter as it happened, luckily keeping my finger on the remote shutter throughout the sequence.

DAVID CLAPP

'Detonate', Land's End, Cornwall, England

In March 2008, an extreme low-pressure weather system pushed its way to English shores from the mid-Atlantic. With a deafening roar, 75ft-high waves eerily arched almost in slow motion, pounding the cliffs at Land's End with unstoppable magnitude. The human race loves to fraternise with danger and many people, myself included, headed to the coast to witness this amazing event. With the tower standing at around 150ft above sea level, a thrill seeker grips the railings screaming with excitement, the force sending spray soaring 250ft into the evening light, before being blown inland by 85mph winds. Next time, I will be in the picture rather than taking it. Unforgettable.

MIKE STEPHENSON ···⇢

Sunrise on Combestone Tor, Dartmoor, Devon, England

This was taken after a frantic drive to get to the Tor for sunrise. After arriving and finding all the usual locations busy, I decided to walk over to this typical moorland tree and try my luck with a High Dynamic Range (HDR) image due to the very wide range of contrast and the inability to use a graduated neutral density filter with the tree taking up such a large part of the shot. The slight mist on the left caught my eye and I think adds to the feeling one often gets on the moors in the early morning.

Judge's choice Jasmine Teer

⚜ PAUL KNIGHT

Coastal barriers, Happisburgh, Norfolk, England

The picture pretty much just took itself; it is one of those shots that one has to be an idiot to get wrong! The clouds were just right, and so was the light. All I really did was set the camera to a long exposure, use a graduated neutral density filter and wait for the right waves to hit the beach. It is carnage on that beach, and looks like a scene after the Normandy landings. It was my third visit and yet again it was the weather conditions and evening light that brought out the spirit of the place.

✞ ADAM BURTON

Looking towards the Cuillins from Elgol, Isle of Skye, Scotland

Sometimes photography trips can be disappointing. A friend and I had returned from what could be described as an unsuccessful Scottish highland trip – it rained virtually the whole week. However, every so often something special happens and this trip included several of these moments. Our first evening on the Isle of Skye provided some of the most special lighting I have been fortunate to photograph. This one shot, for me, made the whole week-long trip worthwhile. I'm not ashamed to say that I love this shot. All the elements seem to work so well together; the brooding sky, the glow on the horizon, the layered mountains, the glowing foreground rocks, the crashing waves. It was only the briefest of moments in which the light glowed yet something that I will remember forever.

NEIL WILLIAMS

Battersea Power Station from Victoria, London, England

I've photographed Battersea Power Station hundreds of times, but this unusual view from Victoria Station is my favourite. It was a hot, stormy August evening and just starting to rain with a low sun just catching the chimneys. The clock in the picture reads 20.55.

🌲 RICHARD JOHNSON

Am Monadh Dubh, West Highlands, Scotland

A frozen Lochan na h'Achlaise at my feet, I was losing the battle to keep warm while waiting for the pink sherbet colours to appear pre-sunrise. I had visualised this view so many times before, only to be disappointed. On this occasion, lady luck was on my side.

✝ **WALTER LEWIS**

Luskintyre Bay, Isle of Harris, Scotland

This was my first visit to the Hebrides, so it was with real anticipation that I approached Luskintyre Bay. Once there, under a blue sky and white clouds, it just wasn't doing anything for me. So it was that I found myself in the sand hills and engrossed in 'making do' with patterns on the sand from the windblown tips of marram grass. After an hour or so, I suddenly became aware of something looming... an area of thick, dark cloud was sweeping rapidly across the bay, and in front of it the sun shone brightly. Ten hectic minutes later the light show was all over... but I'd got my shots!

Lowepro Award for BEST ENVIRONMENTAL image (Adult)

🌱 JOE BOWES

Four trees, Broughton, Oxfordshire, England

Black-and-white has an uncanny way of creating contrast and drama out of something initially unseen. At first sight, this harvested rape field in late autumn was very scrubby and not that attractive, but imagining the light grasses as white and the green scrub as black revealed a distinctive pattern. Framing the four trees just over the brow of the hill and filtering the sky balanced and graduated the image.

GARY McPARLAND

Giant's Causeway at sunset, County Antrim, Northern Ireland

This was taken at the Giant's Causeway in June while I was on a weekend photography trip with some friends. The weather was very uninspiring but for a short while, before sunset, the clouds parted and we were treated to some nice light.

BAXTER BRADFORD ⋯⟩

'Elemental elegance', Dorset, England

The Dorset coast offers a wonderful variety of moods throughout the day and is an enthralling place to spend time, either with a camera or just to be there and enjoy the magnificence of nature. In this winter pre-dawn scene, the rocks shimmer as the sea proceeds with its slow form of water sculpture.

MIKE BREHAUT

St Martin's Point, Guernsey

This is a favourite spot of mine; the small white building is a foghorn, accessible from a small concrete bridge. Being stuck out in the strong currents of Guernsey's south east coast ensures an almost year-round pounding from the Atlantic swells. After many visits, this one morning all of the elements I could have wished for came together, the strong swell, golden dawn light and an approaching storm. Only when I arrived home did I spot the bonus seagull in the top left corner completing this sea view.

IAN CAMERON ⋯⃗

A ruined bothy at Kinloch Hourn, Scotland

Kinloch Hourn lies at the end of surely one of the most beautifully scenic dead ends in Britain. The landscape changes from enclosed deciduous woodland to serene lochs to tumbling waterfalls and wide-open vistas throughout its 22-mile length. I have stopped at this little collapsed stone bothy before and when I arrived there this time it was raining but the intensity of autumn colour was dazzling. The grey, thunderous sky actually served to exaggerate the colours that were further enhanced by the soaking the foliage had received. I added a polariser to remove the surface reflections from the leaves and grasses which made the colours sing, but the icing on the cake was the peppering of light that painted luminous streaks across the upper hills, turning a pretty scene into a majestic classic landscape.

◆⋯ KATE BARCLAY

Summer storm, Cromer, Norfolk, England

A big stormy sky, late one summer's evening. I'd had a frustrating day at work and was desperate to get out with my camera. I headed for Cromer beach where a fantastic storm was brewing overhead. The waves were enormous and the light was great. I was in seventh heaven – lost in the atmosphere of the moment doing what I enjoy most.

59

ALAN YOUNG

Hornsea, East Yorkshire, England

I had gone for a walk with my family for some fresh air. The sky was extremely ominous and it was threatening to rain any second. We were retreating to the car, when the stone in the sand caught my eye. I quickly crouched down in the wet sand and took three images in succession. The water receding on the sand created a mirror reflection beautifully. The heavens opened shortly after taking this shot.

IAN CAMERON

'Jacob's Ladders', Rannoch Moor, near Glencoe, Scotland

This iconic island tree can be viewed on desolate Rannoch Moor from the A82 as it wends its way towards the stunning mountains of Glencoe. On the day I was passing, the conditions were about as unpromising as you can imagine, horizontal rain and grey skies; a typical summer's day in fact. However, I noticed one or two shafts of light striking hills to the extreme left and concluded that this was probably a storm about to pass by so I stopped and walked back to the roadside viewpoint. I hoped that the shafts of light might approach and illuminate the tree directly but instead I was lucky enough to see something much more unusual. The light fell behind the tree and illuminated a strip of grass, turning it emerald green. The tree, which had previously merged with the backdrop of grey mountains, now stood out in stark silhouette, giving me a most unusual take on a familiar scene.

✝ ADAM SALWANOWICZ

Late afternoon at Loch Etive, Scottish Highlands

A cloudy and rainy afternoon during my second trip to Scotland didn't promise much but I decided to stick to my plan and visit Loch Etive anyway. When I finally arrived at the lake I couldn't believe my eyes. The wind had died, low evening sunrays covered the mountains with warm light and the air was crystal clear. It was like entering another world. I knew this paradise would not last long. I chose a panoramic composition, checked the settings three times and made the shot. 15 minutes after I arrived, the sun was gone, heavy cloud rolled over and wind broke the perfect mirror of the lake surface. No surprise there. After all, it was late February.

✣ ADRIAN BICKER

Fields of rape near Weymouth, Dorset, England

I have admired the shape of this field beside the main road to Weymouth for many years. I love its gentle slopes and the clean lines of its boundaries, leading to the group of trees that breaks the horizon. All the elements came together with a crop of oilseed rape in the main field and another behind the trees, set off by the fresh green of newly germinated cereal crops all around. Late morning put the sun at right angles to the view and coincided with the appearance of fair weather cumulus clouds, adding interest to a plain blue sky. This is the first cloud of the day but others are closing in from the right, casting their long shadows across the undulating green fields. I always find this image uplifting. It seems so positive, so vibrant and uncomplicated. So optimistic!

⬅ IAN CAMERON

Hoar-frosted stubble fields at dusk, Aviemore, Cairngorm, Scotland

I was travelling home with my wife and two young children on Boxing Day, when I happened across this gorgeous winter scene with honey-coloured light spilling beneath mottled clouds, striking the short blades of frozen corn stubble. The sky was simply sublime and I begged my wife for a few minutes to photograph it. I decided to emphasise the wonderful sky and make it a significant part of my composition. While I set up the camera, an elderly gentleman approached and informed me that I was wasting my time and had arrived too late, as the sky had been clear all day. He then ambled across the field and disappeared, hunched against the cold. I confess I was mystified, but I returned to the car an hour and ten rolls of film later grinning from ear to ear like a Cheshire cat.

⬆ STEVEN WESTLAND

The Dome in fog, London, England

Getting this shot involved a huge amount of luck. It was the second foggy day in a row and I'd taken my camera to work on the off-chance of some atmospheric river shots. It was so cold that I had to warm the battery by hand to get enough power to take this shot – the battery died immediately. I was distraught! Luckily it recorded a single good frame.

STEVE BARKER

Field of bales, South Downs, West Sussex, England

This photo was taken at Long Furlong Farm, just below Black Patch Hill, on the South Downs in West Sussex. As the storm was approaching I was waiting for a break in the clouds and for the low evening sun to break through and light the field of bales.

PAUL KNIGHT

Blackfriars Bridge and the River Thames, London, England

I have walked past the columns at Blackfriars often and not seen a shot there, but, on this particular day, all of the conditions worked together and it felt as if it would just disappear again if I didn't take the picture quickly. Everything fell into place; the hardest part was getting the train central. A train crosses the bridge every few minutes and it was a bit like shooting plastic ducks at the fair! 20 minutes after I took the shot, the light and clouds faded and the moment had gone.

MIKE BONSALL ⋯⟩

Castle Cornet, St Peter Port, Guernsey

A long exposure captured the cool, blue tones of dusk and the lights illuminating the castle half an hour after sunset. I used the lines of the steps to lead the eye out toward the lighthouse on the end of the breakwater.

Judge's choice Charlie Waite

NEIL MacGREGOR

Dunstanburgh Castle, Northumberland, England

Dunstanburgh Castle lies at the southern end of Embleton Bay in Northumbria. This classic view is normally taken at sunrise with the castle ruins in silhouette and dramatic red skies dominating the scene. I arrived at the beach at around 8pm in early April, just before sunset. I set my tripod at its minimum height to avoid my shadow being in the frame. I knew that good depth of field would be important to get all the boulders in sharp focus. A shutter speed of around one second achieved this. The receding tide had left the large boulders wet and reflective, which helped to give the glowing effect. The light only lasted for a few seconds before the sun dropped below the horizon – luckily I managed two exposures before the magical effect had gone.

JON TAINTON

Rannoch Moor, Scottish Highlands

A late winter's morning in the Scottish Highlands on Rannoch Moor, where breaking cloud provided an interplay of light and shadow over the snow covered flanks of Meall Tionail, Clach Leathad, Creag an Fhirich and across the vast expanse of the boulder strewn undulating moorland. The monochromatic backdrop of Black Mount juxtaposes with the russet colours of the moorland flora, highlighting the cold beauty of this landscape, with rocks of volcanic origin and landforms sculpted by the last Ice Age.

DAVID J WHITE

The Manger and Dragon Hill, Uffington, Oxfordshire, England

This is a site I know well as I live just down the road in Wantage. It's probably more famous as the site of the ancient chalk carving of the Uffington White Horse but it is The Manger with Dragon Hill on the right-hand side (where legend says that St George slew the dragon) that has always attracted me. This picture was taken on a warm, clear August afternoon when the clouds were bubbling up creating a wonderful sky, with the resultant shadow patterns crossing the landscape.

GRAHAM McKENZIE-SMITH

Glencoe, Scottish Highlands

This is a classic viewpoint of Glencoe, where the A82 turns into the centre of the glen between the towering peaks of the Three Sisters on the left (with the summit of Bidean nam Bian peaking between them) and the famous Aonach Eagach ridge on the right. The road is usually filled with tourists, cars and cargo trucks but I was fortunate on this spring day to have a clear road. I waited for a vehicle to come and was rewarded with a single motorbike whose lone rider somehow enhanced the minute scale of man in this desolate and rugged landscape.

✝ **MIKE BREHAUT**

'Inferno', Bordeaux slipway before dawn in September, Guernsey

I arrived early, as my plan was to record the golden sunrise warming up the cold stone slipway. I could see a thin, red band of cloud in the early morning sky and as dawn approached it increased in intensity until the horizon appeared to be melting into a liquid inferno. This was an amazing morning, one I will never forget.

✝ WAYNE SHIPLEY

'Ingleborough isolation', North Yorkshire, England

Although originally a family outing, I went with the expectation of capturing some dramatic images. We were around the midpoint of our ascent of Ingleborough, clambering over limestone crags, loose scree and walls that made things very difficult. This was definitely not the tourist trail, as we had taken a wrong turning, but knew the direction we had to go, it was just a case of getting back on the defined track. We managed to get over the worst of it and then completely by accident came across this beauty. Ingleborough was directly behind, as I didn't want the sheer scale of the peak in the background to distract from the isolated tree. The crevices gouged out between the rocks were quite deep, several feet in parts, which made balancing awkward. Upon reaching the summit of Ingleborough around an hour later we could look down and see this lonely tree, isolated against all the elements.

PAUL CORICA

The Cuillins from Elgol, Isle of Skye, Scotland

This is the perfect location to get a great view of the Cuillin mountain range on the Isle of Skye. Skye has some of the most dramatic light I've ever encountered and this day was no exception. The beach at Elgol is strewn with colourful rocks and these were used to provide foreground interest in this low-angle shot of the Cuillins. An exposure of four seconds was used to record the movement of foam on the waves in the foreground. 'Elemental' is how I would sum up Skye in one word and, for me, this image conveys the elements of this location well.

⚜ ROSS ARMSTRONG

Looking back to Cramond Island, Firth of Forth, Scotland

On a summer's evening, as I was leaving Cramond Island near Edinburgh, I looked back and was immediately captivated by the sky and its reflection in the pools left behind by the tide. I was also drawn to the sunset in the west that was warming up the horizon and catching the old concrete pillars that lined the causeway. It took me a couple of shots in the evening breeze before I got it right, but in the end everything came together as the wind dropped, the ripples on the water settled and I lined up my polariser and angled my graduated neutral density filter towards the setting sun.

MALCOLM BLENKEY

The Cleveland Hills above a winter fog bank, North Yorkshire, England

I was making my way back home from Stokesley in North Yorkshire with the fog in the valley reducing visibility to about a hundred feet. However, I could see above me that the sun was breaking through the fog in places. To gain some height, I drove to Gribdale and walked up to a viewpoint on Easy Moor adjacent to the Captain James Cook monument. The view was stunning with the whole valley shrouded in fog as the sun was setting in the west. The fog was running down the gulleys off the Cleveland Hills to pile even more vapour into the valley below. Underneath this fog bank are the villages of Stokesley and Great Ayton and, just out of image, Roseberry Topping was eerily poking through the veil of fog.

PETER RIBBECK ⋯⟩

Ardrossan High Road, West Kilbride, Scotland

This was taken in the early morning on the Ardrossan High Road. The mist was rolling in and was giving a lovely diffused glow. It was very cold (-5°c) and it was a bit of a shock to leave the confines of my nice warm car. My hands were cooling down quickly and I fumbled with the setting of my camera. I used the tree to help shield my lens from the sun and used the road as a lead-in.

⚕ JASON THEAKER

'Against all odds', Brimham Rocks, North Yorkshire, England

Nature has a magical ability to find ways of surviving in adverse circumstances. It is happening all around us and we all too often fail to reflect on the positive lessons it offers us. I myself am guilty of this and need to consciously remind myself that 'life is good', even when it seems misled by unwanted influences. I wish I could live in the 'now'; you see so much more, smell so much more, hear so much more, appreciate so much more. From time to time, I get glimpses of the 'now', but not often enough!

PHILIP SEARLE

Early evening at Lacock, Wiltshire, England

This photograph was taken on the road leading to the medieval bridge near Lacock Abbey in Wiltshire, the home of photographer William Fox Talbot, during the heavy rains and floods of July 2007. The River Avon, that runs near the village, had burst its banks flooding the grounds of the Abbey, the nearby roads and the fields beyond. With the heavy clouds still present overhead, I've tried to capture the dark mood of the time, tone mapping the image to enhance the feeling of devastation the floods had brought to the area.

SIMON BERRY

Bushy Park in the snow, Richmond upon Thames, Surrey, England

I woke up early one morning in April to see it had been snowing during the night. I know Bushy Park well and knew I could get some good photos of the untouched snow if I got there early enough that morning. When I arrived there, I saw the oak tree with snow on its branches against a white sky and just loved the simplicity of the view in front of me.

RICHARD EDWARDS

The Clifton Suspension Bridge, Bristol, Avon

The quintessential view of Bristol – the Avon Gorge and the Docks, with the Georgian splendour of Clifton and Brunel's Suspension Bridge above. This shot was a challenge and was taken on my eighth trip to do it. Despite all the modern kit that enabled me to combine exposures, it was a tricky job. One botched element and the picture would be ruined. While a far cry from my Grandad's plate camera, I find that this technique captures realistically what you would actually see if you had been standing with me on the banks of the Avon.

·←· DAV THOMAS

Penmon lighthouse and Puffin Island, Anglesey, Wales

Rarely does one of my images take me back so vividly to the feeling I had when I pressed the shutter – a perfectly calm July evening with the sea slowly erasing all the plant life around me, soon leaving only the dominant and beautiful features of my favourite lighthouse at Penmon and its neighbour, Puffin Island.

·T· PETER BIRCH

Dent Head Viaduct, Cumbria, England

I have long been fascinated by viaducts and the way they sit in the landscape; rigid, linear and geometric, the antithesis of their surroundings. Yet somehow, they always look like they belong.

✝ RON WALSH

A spring evening in Falkland, Fife, Scotland

On the day of taking this image, I had spent a couple of hours in the morning searching for something that caught my eye. Having discovered this recently ploughed field, I made the decision to return that evening, hoping for a sunset and some cloud. On this occasion I was fortunate enough to get both. The hill in the background is East Lomond that lies beside the historic town of Falkland in Fife. I initially set up my tripod outside the fence line, but quickly moved inside to the margin of the field to get a better angle on the rows of newly prepared stitches as well as to give more prominence to East Lomond in the picture. Overall, a thoroughly enjoyable hour or two spent on my knees in a field.

TIM PARKIN

Before the morning, Brimham Rocks, North Yorkshire, England

For a couple of months, my wife, Charlotte, and I would take the hour's drive to Brimham
Rocks every Saturday at around 5am. Having navigated by torchlight and found a perch
that looked over this fantasy stage set, we would sit with our flasks of tea and coffee,
eat breakfast and wait for the light to arrive. On this morning, a faint glow on the horizon
gradually brought a fantasy scene to life and the frost and mist lent it all a mystical glow.
Although I now have a variety of different sunrises captured from this location, it is this
pre-dawn glow that I keep coming back to. I often get asked why on earth anyone would
get up that early in the morning just to take a photograph – this photograph is now my
standard response.

MATT KEAL

Duart Castle, Isle of Mull, Scotland

I went to visit the Isle of Mull of the west coast of Scotland, having been inspired by a BBC documentary from wildlife film-maker Gordon Buchanan, called 'Eagle Island'. Although I don't generally get involved in wildlife photography, I was excited by the breathtaking landscape Mull had to offer. As a commercial photographer, any landscape work I get involved in tends to be aimed at the tourist industry, requiring sun and blue skies. The weather on Mull changes every hour it seems, but there is no shortage of dense cloud and stormy skies. I have to admit that luck played its part with regard to light and atmosphere when I came across the view, as I only had to wait for about half an hour before I was happy. The castle dominates that part of the coastline and the highland cattle, for me, added the perfect Scottish signature. I never knew this view was on Mull before visiting the Island, it was simply one of a thousand pictures this beautiful corner of the world has to offer.

⚜ REBECCA CUSWORTH

Eilean Donan Castle and Loch Duich, Scotland

Eilean Donan Castle is a true Scottish icon and, as I stood facing the view that has been photographed by countless tourists, I realised it would be difficult to capture something really original. I could see the storm clouds gathering overhead and, feeling the tension in the air, I knew I had to work quickly before the sky broke and any chance of capturing the stillness of the loch would be lost. A change in perspective would be crucial to creating a unique view so I chose this angle that enabled me to harness the heavy cloud cover and make the most of the beautiful reflection on the Loch's surface. Yellow hues were subdued during post work to make this castle look even less like a tourist trap and more like the foreboding defensive structure it was in the 9th century.

⟵ LIAM LESLIE

Open field, Ullswater, Lake District, England

Taken on a recent trip to the Lake District, I found this view while walking around Ullswater.

⟶ ELOISE ADLER

Silverdale sunset, Lancashire, England

This photo was taken at Silverdale on Morecambe Bay at sunset in May. I took three exposures; for the sky, water pools, and the foreground, and then combined them afterwards. I love the colours, and also the way the arrow-shaped pool in the foreground points into the photo, toward the hills.

LIVING THE VIEW
adult class

LIVING THE VIEW ADULT CLASS WINNER

⟨···· JASON INGRAM

Gardening at first light, Devon, England

This shot was taken at 5am as the sun rose from behind the hills at Bertie's Cottage, Devon. The gardener, Patti O'Brien, is up with the lark most mornings during the summer months, tending her vegetable plot and enjoying the golden light. As she says, 'This really is the most beautiful time of the day, so silent and full of anticipation'.

LIVING THE VIEW ADULT CLASS RUNNER-UP

KEVIN WALSH ···⊱

Grounded ferry at night, Blackpool beach, Lancashire, England

This 6,041 tonne, 380ft-long (116m), Ro-Ro ferry was grounded on Blackpool beach, Lancashire, after being hit by a freak wave in storm force 10 winds on 31 January 2008. The ship had been sailing to the port of Heysham from Warren Point in Northern Ireland. Twenty three people were on board, including four passengers. RAF helicopters rescued everyone and no injuries were reported. The photo was taken at about 7pm on a night in early February after all the sightseers had gone, leaving just one solitary walker on the deserted beach.

DAVID DAGGAR

Riding the sea breeze, Bantham, Devon, England

I was attracted, not only by the evening light, but also by the fact that I could view the kite surfer from a nearby clifftop. This high viewpoint meant that, unusually, I could include the surfer with his kite against the background of a dark cliff in shadow.

ANDREW MIDGLEY

Summer storm, Holkham, Norfolk, England

This shot was originally going to be all cloud, beach and sea, and then the joggers appeared which made the composition work and gave the shot scale. I got completely soaked minutes later.

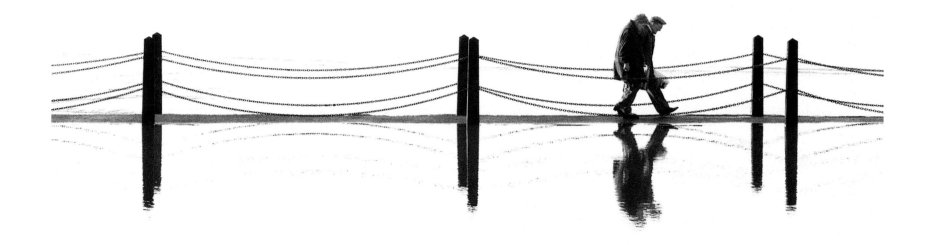

✝ **ALEX WOLFE-WARMAN**   HIGHLY COMMENDED

Couple on causeway, Weston-super-Mare, Somerset, England

I was out making photographs on Weston seafront at around 7.30am. It was a beautiful, crisp and misty morning. I had made a few frames of the seafront and Marine Lake and was about to move on when I noticed this couple walking down the steps towards the causeway. I positioned myself so I could take the shot as they walked through the central part of the causeway. I had time to make two photographs as they walked past; this is the second and my favourite of the two.

Ballintoy, Northern Ireland

While visiting Ballintoy, on the north coast of Antrim, I noticed some sort of religious service going on high up on the bank just beside the little harbour. I realised this would make for a great photo opportunity as the ceremony adds a slightly bizarre touch to the magnificent scenery. The white robed figures added an interesting 'human' element, with great visual impact against the powerful backdrop of crashing waves. A higher point of view best captured the huge waves crashing in around the group. In this particular frame, it looks like the sea was dividing and rising up as described in the book of Psalms.

Psalm 78:13 *"He divided the sea and caused them to pass through, And He made the waters stand up like a heap."*

Judge's choice Tracy Hallett

⚕ IAN McDONALD

Paraglider at dusk, Firth of Clyde, Scotland

A paraglider flying from Kaim Hill, Fairlie, at dusk on a summer evening. The islands of Little Cumbrae, Bute and Arran are seen in the background with the Kintyre peninsula beyond.

✝ ANDY McGREGOR

Dawn flight from Beinn Alligan, Torridon, Scotland

It seemed like a daft idea to paraglide from the summit of Beinn Alligan in mid-winter. We had a long, cold trudge up the hill in the dark but were rewarded with the most amazing sunrise. Heart still pounding from the walk, I just had time to snatch this shot of my friend Mark before I lobbed off too.

✝ DAVID BROOKER

Beachy Head, East Sussex, England

Illustrating the dangers of getting close to the edge of a very unstable cliff.

✝ JOHN MARTIN

The path to St Sunday Crag, Cumbria, England

Just a perfect day – taking a rest on the steep path that climbs up to St Sunday Crag. Looking
north over Patterdale Common to a perfect blue sky reflected by Ullswater and the challenge
of Place Fell waiting for another day.

✝ **RICHARD BURDON**

BMX Boys, Whitby Pier, North Yorkshire, England

I went to Whitby one summer's evening, intending to shoot a variation on the classic Whitby pier shot. The weather was lovely, but slightly cloudy, so I waited for a while, then set up my tripod and waited for the sun break through the clouds to illuminate the pier. After an hour and a quarter, I was starting to get bored and considering going to the pub. I'd been watching some boys mucking about on BMX bikes, practising jumping off the steps, when one of them came up to me and said, 'Take my picture mister?' I reluctantly agreed, opened up the aperture on my camera and started shooting. This image was the best of about 40 frames taken in around 10 minutes and for me, it really captured the moment.

PETER SPECK ⋯⋯⋗

Scafell the hard way, Cumbria, England

I always carry a camera when climbing and have developed a system over the years to safely take pictures while belaying. On this occasion, my friend and I were on Moss Ghyll Grooves, a very severe route high on the main Scafell buttress. The mist conceals the extreme exposure of the situation, hundreds of feet above the valley of Wasdale in the English Lake District. An hour or so later, when we finally completed the route, we emerged out of the gloom and entered a magical world of sunshine and big skies. Not far away, scores of walkers were completing their journey in shorts and tee shirts to the summit of England itself.

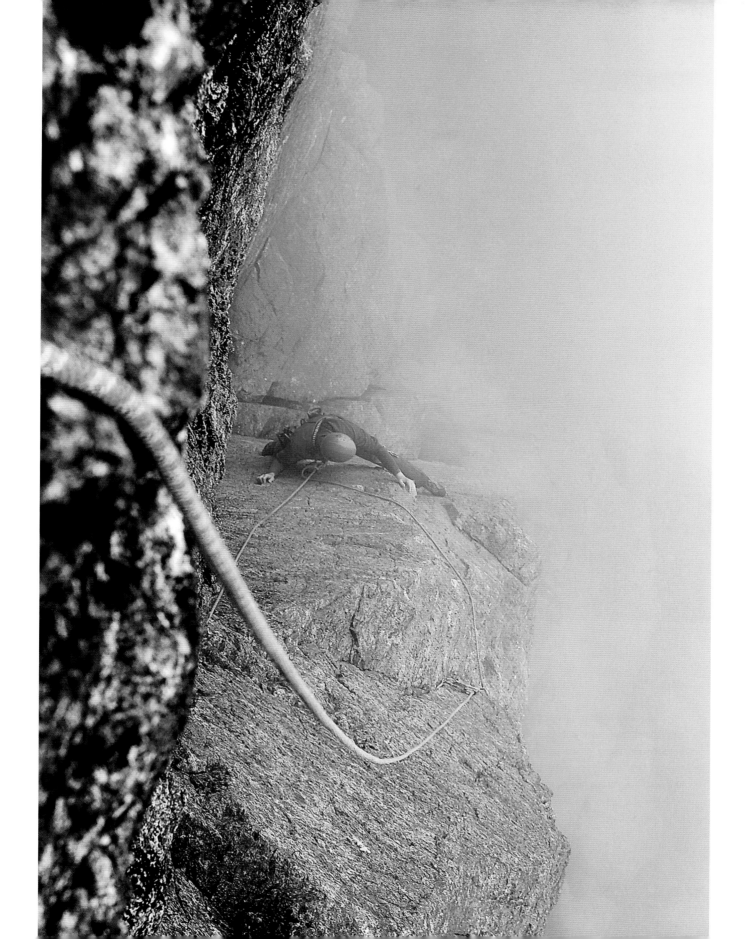

PETER STEVENS

Early morning run, Ullswater, Cumbria, England

This image was taken on an October morning by Ullswater in the Lake District. The lighting was fantastic; so exciting. It took a little while to compose, moving the tripod up and down, left and right, trying to keep a separation between the various elements. While doing so, the runner came by and I remember thinking I'd missed him. I then completed the composition and was about to take the picture when the runner again entered the viewfinder. Perfect.

🕆 **ANDREW JONES**

Path to Pen-y-Fan, Brecon Beacons National Park, Wales

After a heavy mid-winter fall of snow, I had got to the top of Corn Du by dawn to savour and photograph the pristine snow-covered mountain landscape before anyone else was around. By mid-morning, a steady stream of walkers could be seen appearing from the mist-covered valley below, walking up the same path I had used myself a few hours earlier.

ALEX WALLACE

Bass angler Brian Montgomery at sunset, Rocquaine Bay, Guernsey

It was a perfect summer evening but, without a cloud in the sky. I'd not anticipated taking any photographs – until I spotted this lone fisherman casting a lure for bass. His silhouetted form stood out boldly against the pastel hues of sea and sky. I sat crouched in the water for half an hour shooting frame after frame and, as the sun dropped, so the wind died. The sea stilled to a mirror calm sheen – completing the picture perfectly.

JONNY THOMPSON

Sly on Lake, Loch Lomond, Scotland

The shot was taken early one morning in September, with the mist rising over Loch Lomond. It was totally silent – not surprising with nobody to be seen for miles around. The light was very flat and even, quite typical for this part of the world. Loch Lomond is a place of quiet, solitude and space, yet still has an intense atmosphere all of its own.

ANDREW TOBIN

A quiet walk, West Wittering, West Sussex, England

A solitary gentleman takes a walk along a deserted West Wittering beach on a fresh, cold March afternoon.

SIMON KENNEDY ···>

Snape Maltings, Suffolk, England

Taken on a fairly nasty day in winter with stormy weather bringing a sky that was, at times, very dramatic. A fantastic place for photography, interesting architecture and history, and photogenic decay. I like the way the position of the slightly mysterious figure seems to anchor the composition, and how the other elements seem to fly up through the arches to the timber bridge that sails over. There were many interesting details and tones in this image, and it really worked so much better as a monochrome than as a colour image.

PHIL JONES

Walking on Borth Beach at sunset, Wales

Borth Beach, on the Ceredigion coast, is a wonderful stretch of sand extending from the cliffs in the south to the sand dunes of Ynyslas in the north. At low tide the beach reveals the hidden landscape of the submerged forest. Being west-facing, the colours in the beach come alive at sunset. The walkers with their dog are the main attraction in this picture with the bird on the breakwater adding the final touch.

GRAHAM SMITH

Caswell Bay, Gower, Wales

When friends from Salisbury visited us at Easter, we headed down to Caswell for the afternoon with the aim of walking around the clifftop to Langland Bay. The children were exploring the rock pools and climbing on the rocks around the Bay and I was taking pictures of both them and the beach in general. Hollie was fascinated by the many starfish in the pools and pulled this one out for a closer look. The weather was quite overcast and we got caught in a rain shower while on the headland between the two bays. Hot chocolates in Langland Cafe helped warm us up.

Winner of the Visit Wales Award

CHRIS FRIEL

Whitstable, Kent

This was taken on an October afternoon, while walking the children home from school. I'd bought a new camera that day, so took a few shots of them running around on the beach.

✝ DAVID BAKER

Entertaining the Covent Garden crowds, London, England

London's Covent Garden attracts entertainers and tourists from all over the world. The artists are unpaid for their work and rely on donations from the crowds that form around the West Piazza. I managed to position myself behind the entertainer and shooting with a wide-angle lens meant I had to get quite close to him in order to include the crowd in the frame. I remained in position for most of his performance. However, when he stripped down to a pair of orange hot pants and fired up the chainsaw I knew it was time to move on, and I did so after throwing a fiver in his hat.

⚕ BEN EVANS

Self-portrait, Bristol, England

This was taken on a walk around a virtually empty Bristol on Boxing Day morning. The soft light from an overcast sky revealed detail in the ground, and I thought it a good opportunity for a self-portrait of sorts; the silhouette hopefully makes this appear unlike the cliché of photographer's self-portrait-with-camera, which I suppose it is, really.

GEOFFREY LAUDER ·····⋗

Hunstanton Beach, Norfolk, England

This was taken at the height of the holiday season, portraying people silhouetted on the beach. I was attracted by the person flying a colourful kite, together with the brilliant stratas of light and shade across The Wash.

PAUL TURNER

Landing the catch, Hastings, East Sussex, England

On a bitterly cold late afternoon in January, a small fishing boat approaches the beach to unload its catch, as a member of the shore crew waits to attach a line to haul the boat up the steep shingle. With the light fading fast and a dramatic winter sky, the figure stands patiently in semi silhouette against a leaden sea allowing a few moments to compose the image. A moment of concentration is captured in anticipation of the tricky task of plunging into freezing water to secure the cable.

BILL ALLSOPP

Weybourne beach, near Holt, Norfolk, England

I was staying a few miles away near Holt and rose early to visit this beach at dawn. I had already been during the day some time earlier and thought that it may have prospects on an autumn dawn with the sun rising just out to sea, but did not know quite what to expect. What a morning! Glorious light, a mackerel sky and just one fishing boat to be launched for a day's work. Sometimes you can go out and get nothing; this morning produced three cracking images. I used to be content if I got one good image in a roll of 36, three in half an hour is quite exceptional!

✞ COLIN CADLE

Relaxing on the beach at Beer, Devon, England

Out with my new camera on a wonderful September afternoon, it was impossible to pass by these perfectly backlit deckchairs and their sole occupant without making an image.

☩ RICHARD HARRIS

Woolacombe beach, Devon, England

Woolacombe has a three-mile long stretch of golden sand that I thought would be a great location for my 40th birthday weekend away with family and friends.

It was a warm, hazy Saturday morning and the beach didn't seem like a good idea straight away but around midday there was an excitement on the beach; something you could hear but not see. My camera is an extension of my arm, whatever the conditions... you never know! Like a kid in a sweet shop; as the mist cleared with the sun directly above, the stage was set. Within five minutes it looked like a normal day. The photograph has a very calming feel, with an element of excitement in the air. With, 'brush stroke'-like reflections, each ghost-like figure seemed to be dancing on ice; a perfect day at the beach.

GARY EASTWOOD

Jogger on Hove promenade in April snowstorm, East Sussex, England

It is unusual to have snow at all on the South Coast, but even more so in April when this image was taken. Waking up to a freak snowstorm, I grabbed my camera and went straight out. On reaching the promenade this was the first scene to confront me, and I couldn't believe that anyone would be jogging in those conditions. The classic 'beach hut' shot has been taken so many times, but because snow is so rare here I hope this offers a slightly different take on it. Unfortunately, I stayed out too long and got damp in my camera, which needed repairing!

MARK SADLIER

Brighstone Forest, Isle of Wight, England

The couple in the picture weren't going to be put off their Sunday morning walk and pushed their buggy valiantly through the unusual April snowfall.

⋖⋯ **ANDREW BARTON**

Menai Straits at sunrise, North Wales

This shot was taken about an hour after sunrise on the Menai Straits, looking to Bangor Pier. After many failed visits to this location, all the elements came together on this morning.

MALCOLM KAY

Isle of Skye, Scotland

Loch Sligachan and Glamaig, from an ascent of Am Basteir in the Cuillin of Skye, under April snow.

PAUL SANDY ⋯⟩

On Chesil Beach, Dorset, England

I took this in June 2008 on a photographic trip to Dorset. It was a sweltering hot afternoon and I left most of the group by the shoreline to get a drink from the shop before it shut. As I slipped and crunched my way up the steep bank of pebbles at the top of the beach, I saw these sunbathers to my right. I glanced once, then again when I saw that the seagulls on the crest of the ridge were forming an arc that echoed the tops of umbrellas. I made six exposures and headed hastily for the shop. When back home editing the images, I decided that the arrangement of the gulls was most pleasing in this one and that a square crop worked best.

🎣 **TERRY FOSTER**

Fisherman at local pond, South Yorkshire, England

This is a local fishing pond at Darfield, Barnsley; a former coalmine. Taken in the summer, with late evening sun.

🕇 GRAHAM McKENZIE-SMITH

View from Tantallon Castle, East Lothian, Scotland

Taken from the walls of Tantallon Castle, remnant of the Douglas stronghold in East Lothian, looking toward Berwick Law, originally a volcanic plug. The low late-winter sun gave this scene a strangely apocalyptic atmosphere, and the people following the path to the solitary building look like they are seeking the only remaining shelter. The building is actually a dovecot, and quite a large one at that!

⚕ JONATHAN LUCAS

'Go with the wind', Branscombe Beach, Norfolk, England

It was a lovely evening in August. We'd enjoyed strolling around the beach for a few hours and then watched as a storm built steadily and approached the shore. At the time this was taken we could hear the thunder rumbling over the bay, and shortly after we were running for cover as lightning and hail crashed around us in our car. Incredibly, there were people still flying kites at that point! The light was great and the lone man sand-sailing made a stark contrast to the ominous storm clouds. I had wanted the lead-in lines of the groynes to meet with him, but in the end I was happy that they led out of shot towards the only patch of calm weather. The effect of this was to isolate him in the frame still further.

ANTHONY ANGUS

Looking south from the Arrochar Alps, Scotland

On a beautiful morning in January, low pressure rushing up from the south had brought with it a carpet of cloud. This added to the drama of being high up on an amazing mountain landscape in near-perfect winter conditions. Then we had a stunning temperature inversion far below to set it all off. Argyll was strutting its stuff on a day that landscape photographers surely dream of.

✢ MAGGIE McCALL

Rape field in spring, Milton Abbot, Devon

I drove by this sea of rape every weekday to take my little girl to school, and specifically bought this red umbrella for this particular image that was in my mind's eye. The much-used model is my daughter Ellena, who is very patient with her photography-mad Mummy! I only wanted red and yellow in the image and had to choose my viewpoint carefully, then I had to crop as well, to exclude any sky or trees.

❧ JULIE CHAMBERLAIN

Newport, Isle of Wight, England

This photograph was taken at the Isle of Wight Festival. I only decided to go on the spur of the moment but by Saturday afternoon I was so pleased I'd made it. The sun was shining, bands were playing and I had a beer in one hand and my camera in the other! I took lots of pictures but this is my favourite. It was taken on Sunday morning, the day after the Sex Pistols headlined – the calm after the storm! On Monday, many of us decided to take advantage of the great location and explore this beautiful island before returning home. You could spot us mingling with locals and tourists – walking along the lovely coastal paths, sunbathing on the unspoilt beaches and driving through the picturesque towns. It was the perfect way to end a memorable weekend.

✝ **MIKE DOHERTY**

Snowman in Richmond Park, London, England

The snowman was taken while walking in Richmond Park this year when we had a freak snowstorm. It is rare in the south of England to get such a good covering and the sense of humour of the 'builder' inspired the image. A key part too, was the two figures to the right completing the living landscape.

BERNIE BROWN

Fun in the snow, Belfast, Northern Ireland

Local residents having fun in a snowstorm in the grounds of Stormont, Belfast's
Parliament Buildings.

LIVING THE VIEW
youth class

LIVING THE VIEW YOUTH CLASS WINNER

CONNOR MATHESON

Lone tree in Royston, Barnsley, South Yorkshire, England

This is of a tree in a local field, one that I have been to capture a number of times. This time my friend is looking through the wheat field towards the tree. We hung around for quite some time before I got the right combination of sky and wind. I needed the wind to pick up to get movement in the wheat and I like the slightly swirling effect.

✝ **LAURENZ VOGT**

Hampstead Heath, London, England

A family day out on Hampstead Heath. My uncle is an art student and did a good job with the boating lake.

✝ **JESSICA McLAUGHLIN**

Windy beach, Christchurch Harbour, Dorset, England

This picture was taken on a very windy day. The sand was stinging my legs and I was having trouble keeping it off the camera.

YOUR VIEW
adult class

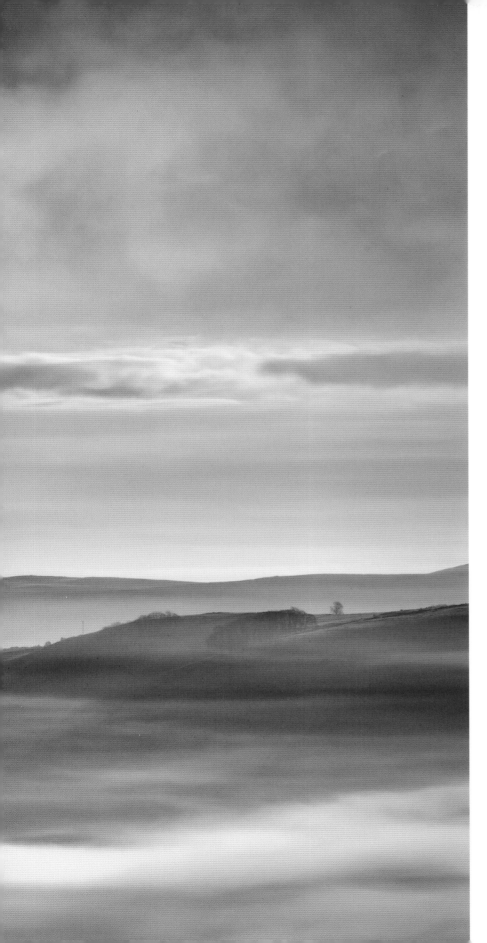

YOUR VIEW ADULT CLASS WINNER

<··· **PETE BRIDGWOOD**

Hope Valley, near Castleton, Derbyshire, England

I had been pre-visualising this image for two years and made no less than five trips to Hope Valley in the Peak District to try and achieve it. Every time I arrived (having carefully timed my visit according to the weather forecasts) I had been met with disappointment – no mist. This particular morning though, I made my image – very satisfying!

YOUR VIEW ADULT CLASS RUNNER-UP

◀··· HOWARD KINGSNORTH

Maunsell Forts, Thames Estuary, England

I hired a boat specifically to visit this location (it's about six miles offshore) with the intention of achieving this and other images, although I was hoping for rougher weather. The location is also the site of an offshore wind farm and I wanted to capture these images as this is a topical subject. I am attracted to land and seascapes in all kinds of weather so this was a natural extension for me.

† **CHRIS CALVER**   HIGHLY COMMENDED

Snowy pier, Southwold, Suffolk, England

When I woke up and saw that it was snowing, I had to get out and capture some snowy
scenes. When I arrived at Southwold, I could hardly see the pier through the blizzard. I set
up my tripod, composed the shot, then waited for a break in the weather. Luckily, after
about half an hour, I was fortunate enough to get the break I wanted. I set the shutter speed,
adjusted the aperture and waited for the right wave.

MARI STERLING

Pwllheli beach, Llyn Peninsula, North Wales

On a late afternoon in February, the sun burst through the clouds for a few minutes, lighting up the scene before me. A half-second shutter speed recreated the illusion of movement in the marram grass. The colourful buildings and gunmetal grey of the sea and sky formed a dramatic backdrop for the foreground sunlit dunes.

KRIS DUTSON

'Give me shelter', Dorset Downs, England

This barn sits high on the Dorset Downs above the hamlet of Wynford Eagle. I wanted to make a photograph that shows the loneliness and exposed position of the barn on top of the hill but also the shelter that it offers. I achieved this by using a long lens to accentuate the hill, leaving a slightly blurred foreground to reveal the valley and add depth. The sun had just come out after a thunder shower, so I used that wonderful storm light raking across the wheat field to highlight the barn and to accentuate the tractor tracks that lead to it.

ROBERT McCALLION

'The Dark Hedges', County Antrim, Northern Ireland

I have been photographing this stunning avenue of ancient beeches for many years. Known locally as 'The Dark Hedges', they are around 300 years old and nearing the end of their natural lifespan. It was early autumn and the setting sun was bathing the branches with soft evening light. The tractor appeared just in time, adding a sense of scale to these magnificent trees. A local trust has been formed to raise funds for their preservation, together with a programme of felling and replanting.

✝ **PETER DOBSON**

Winter storm at Blackpool, Lancashire, England

Taken, crouching by the sea wall, during a force nine gale at high tide from the cliffs at Blackpool. Suddenly backlit, the tower was outlined briefly and yet fogged by the angry spray that filled the hammering air. A moment of madness resulted in a severe drenching, the shot and a hasty retreat.

✝ ROD LEWIS

'Storm at the tin mines', Botallack, Cornwall, England

After a deeply unsatisfying week in Cornwall, in wet and grey conditions, I was about to pack up and leave, feeling depressed, when I came across this place and decided to wait to see if the weather broke. I set up my tripod and framed up, then removed the camera from the tripod and sat in my car to watch a DVD on my laptop. As I did, angry black clouds loomed in and it began to pour with rain. A few hours later, a break in the clouds came suddenly – I don't think I've ever moved so fast! Within minutes, it was bright and sunny for the first time in days and I had to go home! I guess I owe this picture to Alfred Hitchcock, who kept me sitting there!

KATE BARCLAY

'Just caught the light', Portland, Dorset, England

This was taken at the end of a frustrating week in Dorset. I had really struggled to capture an image I was happy with, mainly due to poor weather and never being in the right place at the right time. It was a stormy afternoon when I visited Portland but I was determined to go away with something. I found my shot and just waited for the low light to peak fleetingly through the clouds, hoping it would hit the boat and the huts exactly as I had visualised it.

CHRIS LOGUE ⋯⟩

Control Point, Balgray Reservoir, Scotland

This tower is one of many that dot the public water reservoirs around Scotland. They are relics, reminders of a time when places and resources like this were not automated and controlled from distant computer terminals; but required the physical presence of a trained professional. As such, the nature of these towers required them to be strong, fortified buildings with thick stone turrets and iron spikes. It's these characteristics that invoke other-worldliness, being sinister and hostile in nature. Drawing inspiration from the Iain Banks novel *A Song of Stone* I hope to take the viewer to an alien land, oppressive and out of time. Well-guarded control points pepper the ruined landscape, protecting any remaining resources.

⚕ JOHN POTTER

Burnsall, Wharfedale, North Yorkshire, England

The hoar frost only lasted a couple of hours after sunrise in December, so by 10am it had completely disappeared as a warm front moved slowly north across the Yorkshire Dales National Park.

ROBIN WHALLEY

Merchants Bridge, Castlefield, Manchester, England

The Castlefield area of Manchester is full of wonderful architecture such as Merchants Bridge and the old railway bridge seen here in the background. I decided to shoot the bridge using a combined exposure technique (HDR) as this allowed me get underneath the bridge to gain a fresh perspective, while controlling the high contrast in the image. The low viewpoint also allowed me to show the build-up of grime on the underside of what is otherwise quite a clean modern structure.

PAUL KNIGHT

OXO Tower, River Thames, London, England

I was trying to take a picture of the tower from the jetty, but a security guard told me that I couldn't, as it was private property. So I waited for the tide to go out and set up on the beach. Dark clouds rolled in from the distance and I got the shot. I regret that I couldn't wait for the lights on the tower to come on, but the shot was governed by the tide and the solemn heavy clouds, which had all changed by the time the lights did come on. If I ever see that security guard again I will thank him for helping me get a much better picture than I would have done.

DAVID BARRETT

The Angel of the North, Gateshead, England

This was taken at 4.30am in June, following a four-hour drive north from my Gloucestershire home. Sometimes less is more!

⚐ GORDON SCAMMELL

Walking along the edge, Beachy Head, East Sussex, England

This was my first visit to Beachy Head. The wind was so strong I nearly lost my tripod over the edge! I saw this couple running past and waited until they reached the top of the next cliff. Luckily the third person came into view, as well as a very welcome patch of sunlight.

ADAM BURTON ⋯⋗

'Striving for Perfection', Backley Plain, New Forest National Park, Hampshire, England

I've visited and photographed Backley Plain in the New Forest many times over the years, so on this occasion I was looking for something fresh and new. I decided to move in low and close to two mature oak trees, and chose this unusual composition. I have named this shot *Striving for Perfection* as to me the haphazard yet beautiful branches seem to be reaching out towards the perfectly-formed tree on the horizon.

SIMON KENNEDY

Black Hill near Abergavenny, Wales

I was out walking on Black Hill on a windy and cold winter day, and the sky was very dramatic. I really liked the windswept, bent hawthorn. It gives you some idea of the kind of extreme conditions that can be experienced up in these hills. In the first image I like the way the path leads you down and into the scene. My favourite part of the image is the light rays and light pool just beyond the mid-ground ridge.

In the second image, the hawthorn seems to provide an appropriately craggy foreground and I feel the flares from an old Zuiko 18mm F3.5 lens add to the surreal, fantasy atmosphere.

Judge's choice Nick White

⸙ KEITA YASUKAWA

Millennium Bridge and St Paul's Cathedral, London, England

I initially photographed this image as a part of my ongoing personal project called 'Cranespotting'. After a long period of research and several failed attempts to photograph this, I found out that it would be best shot on a cold night (the later the better, but before dawn) midweek with fine stable weather. I shot 15 frames across from west to east, each frame with a 10 minute exposure. On a cold, clear night, the air is usually crisp and visibility is better. It was really hard to be patient. No one else except me could be on the bridge. So I would just stop taking photos and wait when someone came along. Therefore, each attempt easily took four or five hours.

I had to give up one of the attempts because a couple stopped and never started walking again. Another time, the sun began to rise. Even before it had brightened up, sometimes the early bird joggers were out. Another time, the weather let me down. Another time, the lights at St Paul's Cathedral just switched off. And so on...

It took me almost a year from the initial idea to the night I successfully photographed this image.

Winner of Enjoy England Award

JONATHAN LUCAS ⸽

'Sutcliffe's Apartments', near Arnos Grove, London, England

This pays homage to Frank Meadow Sutcliffe, a famous photographer of North Yorkshire who shot, so emotively, scenes from Whitby and the surrounding area. I went to school for a short while in Stockton-on-Tees, exploring Yorkshire extensively with my family. This viaduct, over which runs the Piccadilly Line, reminded me of the Yorkshire brickwork, the arches forming the many avian homes alluded to in the title. There are always pigeons roosting there and this misty December morning was no exception.

Judge's choice Damien Demolder

RICHARD BURDON

Staithes, North Yorkshire, England

This is a shot that always raises a comment, even people who are familiar with the village struggle to figure out where it was taken from. In fact one local even suggested that it was taken from a helicopter! In reality it was taken from the top of the Cow Bar Nab, where the seagulls roost. I'd been to Staithes a couple of times to see when the light would be right, then returned early one August evening. The light was good, but the sky was cloudy, so I set up and waited for over an hour, only for it to suddenly go dark and pour with rain! Soaking wet and dispirited, I was heading back to the car when the sun broke through the clouds, so I dashed back through the sodden undergrowth to my vantage point and finally got the shot I was looking for.

LES McLEAN ⋯⟩

Paddy's Hole, South Gare, North Yorkshire, England

Paddy's Hole, at South Gare, situated at the mouth of the River Tees, is a popular location for photographers. This gentle backwater seems quaintly old fashioned, with its fishing boats, lobster pots and fishermen's huts, seemingly at odds with the more modern heavy industrial environment surrounding. For this image, taken at dusk, I tried to capture this contrast, using the lights of the steelworks complex as a backdrop to the foreground fishing boats.

MATTHEW JELLINGS

STEEN DOESSING ···⟩

Lake in West Oxfordshire at dawn, England

'Intertidal', Isle of Wight, England

This solitary oak tree remains standing on an island after the land surrounding it was quarried and then transformed into a lake. I've cycled to this location on many occasions, arriving before dawn to capture the sun rising from behind the tree. On this particular morning it was the combination of mist and gentle ripples that inspired me to take the photograph.

With family and work commitments, when I am not on a planned trip, I have to fit shooting in with other obligations and I try to grab every opportunity. This was taken on a family holiday to the Isle of Wight in August. It was late morning, sunny and very hazy.

MIKE BONSALL

The Bathing Pool, St Peter Port, Guernsey

This image was made at dawn on a still mid-summer's morning at 4.30. As the tide fell, it revealed a pool of still water that reflected the sky beautifully. The image, while calming, also has a real sense of drama and tension that I continue to find captivating.

KEITH FOSTER

Big wave at Sandsend, North Yorkshire, England

Taken late evening on a very stormy day with a high spring tide, much damage was done by this wave to the hotel and the cottages on the sea front. It was difficult to take as the high sea was running behind me. Sandsend is in real danger as the seas rise with global warming.

IAN CAMERON

Loch Droma, Strathglass, Scotland

Loch Droma, at an altitude of 1,000 feet, lies beside the A835 Garve to Ullapool road on a high moorland plateau surrounded by mountains. Although the loch is man-managed and dammed at its western end, the eastern side appears entirely natural; the waters envelop tiny island retreats complete with birch trees. I usually pass it by on my way to the Inverpolly reserve, but on this particular November morning it held me spellbound. The birch tree islands drizzled in autumn golds were immersed in thick mist that hung wraith-like over the loch. At sunrise, the surrounding peaks caught the first light and the gentle warmth of the sun caused the mist to lift. I took the shot at the moment the island tree tops poked through the shroud while the rest remained partially concealed.

JOHN PARMINTER

The Wasdale valley, West Cumbria, England

I'd been watching the weather all day over the fells from my office window and it looked promising. I finished work early and headed up Wasdale with enough light left to have a run up the surrounding hills. On my descent the conditions changed dramatically and I thought there could be a photo opportunity. Hastily, I made my way back to retrieve my camera and caught the last of the day's light to make, what I hope, is an alternative view of Wasdale.

⚓ **JAMES OSMOND**

Portland Bill, Dorset, England

The waters off Portland Bill are well known for their maritime disasters. This shot was taken one winter dawn after a stormy night. While the ominous sky and pounding waves reference the nautical danger here, this is balanced by the hope of better weather on the clearing eastern horizon and the comfort of the guiding light.

✝ ADAM SALWANOWICZ

Douglas, Isle of Man

I have visited the Isle of Man for the past five years, always in late spring. I fell in love with this place from the first moment I saw it. Even though the island is generally very photogenic, trying to catch the spirit of some places isn't always easy. This particular morning lacked light, but low, heavy clouds added an interesting mood to the view of Douglas Bay. I decided to use three vertical frames to get the square composition. Against the rules, I placed the horizon in the middle of the frame and used rocks to balance the heavy clouds. A wide-angle lens helped to emphasise the structure of the rocks and its lines leading out towards the Bay.

DUNCAN McMILLAN

Humber Bridge, East Yorkshire, England

The Humber Estuary at high tide in calm weather provides ideal conditions for photography and this occasion was no exception. This night-time shot of the Humber Bridge south tower was taken from the foreshore on the north bank. The stillness of the river creates a mirror-like surface in which the distant lights are reflected. Their colours are accentuated by natural smearing and rippling, an effect enhanced by the long exposure's softening of the water surface.

DAN PRINCE

Humber Bridge at night, East Yorkshire, England

I was photographing a job the next day and so was staying nearby the night before. I saw the bridge when we arrived and thought it would be interesting to get some personal shots instead of sitting in the hotel room watching TV. My assistant and I ventured out to see what angles we could find and came across an industrial estate that, thankfully, gave us access to the view. We stood in the dark for an hour with the brolly above us and captured some great shots of the bridge.

EMMANUEL COUPE

The Fairy Pools, Isle of Skye, Scotland

It was a heavily-clouded November day on the Isle of Skye and I had decided to spend it shooting the Fairy Pools located in the heart of the Cuillin Mountains. The rain was constant and so were the high winds. Despite the heavy weather, I was able to stay almost the entire day under an umbrella and take photographs of many small waterfalls along the Fairy Pools. I found that the dramatic dark clouds were the ideal fit for this location and conveyed the spirit of the Scottish winter landscape well.

⚲ JANET BURDON

The spirit of Whitby, North Yorkshire, England

A photographer friend once described Whitby as an adventure playground for photographers and I couldn't agree more. I think the use of a super wide-angle lens has created a great effect with the clouds almost appearing to explode out of the picture. A combination of capturing the seagull in the corner of the image and the lovely warm evening light gave an image that, for me, sums up the whole character of Whitby.

☝ ZOË HEMSLEY

'Maman' by Louise Bourgeois at Tate Modern, London, England

Taken on a December afternoon, the sky was fantastic. I wanted to emphasise the presence of the spider 'Maman', almost like an alien invader into our world. I took a view from low down shooting upwards, using the wide angle to enhance the leaning in of the tower of the Tate Modern. I have used a grainy effect to make the image surreal, and burnt out some of the highlights near the tower to create an odd sense of light in the sky; maybe something else follows behind the spider?

MATTHEW PARKER ⋯⋗

The Gherkin, London, England

The Gherkin is such an iconic building on the London skyline; it is something I have wanted to photograph for a while now. Earlier this year, I was planning a trip to the capital and wanted to take the opportunity to photograph some classic iconic structures but try to give them my influence. On my visit to the building, I took a variety of shots from different angles using an ultra wide-angle lens to accentuate the shape of the glass. I particularly like the way the reflections have been captured to show the older style buildings against this modern structure.

⚜ MATTHEW PARKER

Castle Cornet, Guernsey

The idea for this image came to me when developing my ideas and skills using High Dynamic Range (HDR) techniques. I originally shot some images of this view with a portrait aspect; not realising just how effective the images would turn out. Once I realised just how great these looked, I wanted to re-shoot to ensure I had a landscape perspective as well. It took some planning to ensure that I had the right height of tide to coincide with the fading light at sunset. Using a variety of long exposures with a tripod-mounted camera enabled me to smooth out the water and capture the finer details of the breakwater, with the eye being led along to the lighthouse. I particularly like the way that the line started by the breakwater continues along the horizon.

✝ **ROBIN WHALLEY**

The Lowry Theatre, Salford Quays, Manchester, England

The Lowry Theatre isn't too far from where I live and I had been meaning to do a sunset shoot for some time. On this particular evening there was a wonderful sunset but I decided to extend my shoot and try some night shots using a combined exposure technique (HDR). The night air was wonderfully clear and while there were a few ripples on the water, the long exposures necessary for the low light conditions made it possible to smooth the water's surface into a calm reflection.

◀··· COLIN CAMPBELL

Green isle sunset, Scotland

These fields in my 'back garden' are often my subject of choice. The different grasses in this barley field offered an interesting composition so all I had to do was wait for the sun to oblige...

195

🌱 **SIMON BUTTERWORTH**

Roots, Loch Lomond, Scotland

I was fascinated by the root structure of this magnificent tree partially submerged in the winter flood waters of Loch Lomond. I couldn't figure out a way to make an image that would do justice to what I was seeing in front of me. As darkness fell and the shadows merged things suddenly seemed to make sense. The lobster cloud emerging from behind the tree added the final surreal touch.

🌱 **SIMON BUTTERWORTH**

Rock detail, Firth of Forth, Scotland

My original idea had been to photograph Bass Rock on the Firth of Forth at dusk but, as the dreary weather rolled in, I realised my plans were going to be thwarted. I decided to go for a walk instead and literally fell over this beautiful miniature rock structure. The incoming tide provided the gauzy shroud. I have since been back to this spot but the tide has buried the rock under tons of shingle.

⊹ DUNG HUYNH

Southwold, Suffolk, England

This photo was taken during late spring, at sunrise, in Southwold. I wanted to capture the foreground rocks, which lead you nicely to the colourful huts in the background. I took advantage of the light from the sun just rising above the sea horizon to illuminate the foreground rocks and the huts in the background.

KEVIN MARSCH

Humber Bridge, south side, East Yorkshire, England

I have taken hundreds of shots of the Humber Bridge and have never been able to capture the sheer scale and impressiveness of it, until I found this gate. The lines and composition just fell naturally into place.

FRANK PAYNE

St Paul's Cathedral and Millennium Bridge, London, England

This photograph was taken just after 5pm on 1 April and I was standing quite a long way out on the banks of the Thames at low tide. I had planned it some weeks earlier so that low tide and the position of the sun coincided. As the sun sets it is obscured by many high buildings to the west and only emerges at the right height and angle for a relatively short time. It was originally taken for a competition that my university department at Oxford, Engineering Science, ran with the theme: Engineering Genius. For this, my intention was to emphasise the best in modern engineering looking back to the best from a previous age.

JOHN FANNING

Dusk at Kimmeridge Bay, Dorset, England

This beautiful place on the Jurassic Coast in Dorset is a delight to photograph. The numerous ledges present any photographer with plenty of foreground interest and stunning compositional choices.

⚑ LEN GREEN

Southwold Pier at sunrise, Suffolk, England

There are many places in the UK to capture the dramatic effects the sun has on the landscape as it creeps over the horizon, but my favourite place has to be the seaside town of Southwold in Suffolk, and more precisely, Southwold Pier. Until recently, this photograph would not have been possible as the pier and the rocks that form part of the sea defences were not there. This goes to show, beautiful landscapes can be created, and the seaside is not just for hot summer afternoons.

† LES FORRESTER

Drax Power Station near Selby, North Yorkshire, England

It was an early start to Drax, the location for the shot, before sunrise but as the sun came up the fog came down. It was a waiting game until it cleared enough to see all the towers. The wait was worth it as the fog that morning became a bonus.

✝ ANDREW DUNN

Woodhead Pass in winter, near Manchester, England

Low cloud billowed up from the valleys and crested the A628 Woodhead Pass near Manchester as the light faded in the twilight sky. Meanwhile, the traffic, crossing the Pennines from Sheffield, pierced through the frosty landscape. This was an opportunistic picture that I couldn't resist taking. As I drove to Manchester last Christmas, I was captivated by the developing light and clouds and knew that I had to capture the scene. Stopping in the first available lay-by, I rushed across the moors to find an appropriate vantage point. Although you will always be stuck in traffic when crossing the Pennines on this route, I still found myself waiting for several minutes before an appropriate queue of vehicles passed to add the light trails. I wasn't wearing full cold weather clobber, so my fingers were quite frozen by the time I took this exposure.

✝ DAVID ENTRICAN

Clifton Suspension Bridge, Bristol, England

Early in the day, the summer sun brings out the colours of the clouds above Clifton Suspension Bridge, spanning the Avon Gorge in Bristol.

KEITH WASS ···⟩

Scarborough from the Castle, North Yorkshire, England

Scarborough Castle offers several great vantage points for photography. Here I wanted to capture the colourful houses at the front of the shot, people on the beach and elsewhere in ones and twos and little groups and the curve of the road from bottom left to top right. The shot takes advantage of the camera's 10x optical zoom. The distance covered in the picture is probably a mile or more, so I was pleased to be able to capture so many visual details, including the famous Grand Hotel and Spa Bridge. Scarborough was Britain's first seaside resort and the first one I was taken to as a lad, so being there always brings back memories.

YOUR VIEW
youth class

YOUR VIEW YOUTH CLASS WINNER

✝ JAMIE RUSSELL

Sunrise, Holywood, County Down, Northern Ireland

This photograph was taken one morning during the winter, just behind my house. I woke up that morning in bed and saw that my curtains were glowing orange. I knew that it was going to be a breathtaking sunrise. I quickly got dressed and rushed to grab my camera. I decided to take the photo from my bathroom window to get a good height and so I would get the right light effect. In the end it turned out to be one of the best photographs I have ever taken.

✝ **ELOISE ADLER**

Sheep on the edge, Surprise View, Derbyshire, England

I saw this sheep standing on the edge at Surprise View in Derbyshire, and thought it would make an interesting photo. I like the contrast between the warm, golden colours in the foreground and the cool, frosty fields in the background. The photo was taken at sunrise in early February.

⚊ ⚌ HARRY TILSLEY

Reflection at Kimmeridge Bay, Dorset, England

I took this photo during an evening shoot at Kimmeridge Bay in Dorset with my Dad. I was experimenting with the effect of getting very close to the rock pool while keeping some of the background landscape in the frame. I cropped the picture to give the panoramic effect, which is a bit like an alien landscape.

Peveril Point, Dorset, England

At the end of May, my Dad and I decided to get up very early to see the sun rise. This photo was taken before the sun actually rose and the long exposure made the sea look almost like mist or clouds. The resulting image was more or less monochrome and very atmospheric.

PHONE VIEW
adult class

PHONE VIEW ADULT CLASS WINNER

⟵ ANDY McGREGOR

Storm Beach, Nairn, Scottish Highlands

While out walking on the beach, the patterns in the sand intrigued me. I was cursing the fact that I hadn't brought my camera so decided to play with my new phone. This image was the result.

PHONE VIEW ADULT CLASS RUNNER-UP

⟵ KEVIN LELLAND

Near Queen's View, Stirling, Scotland

My SLR camera was back in my rucksack and I was heading home on this June evening. As I turned to look back at the lone tree I had been photographing, the sun emerged one last time. I took this last picture of the day with my camera phone.

⚑ COLIN HOSKINS

⚑ COLIN HOSKINS

The Bull Ring shopping area, Birmingham, West Midlands, England

Bluebell woodland near Berkhamsted, Hertfordshire, England

It was a cold and very clear February night. I was with two good friends and we were on our way back from having a great Indian meal. Tony mentioned that the Bullring shopping area was close by and he thought the architecture there was very interesting. We decided to have a look. After parking the car, we went exploring. As I walked past this building, it was shouting out to be photographed! This was the view when I looked up – I'm so pleased that even the many stars are visible in the final image. I really like this chance picture – must go and have a curry more often!

It was a cloudy Sunday afternoon. I was out driving with friends, when we came across this large woodland area of bluebells. We parked the car on the side of the road, and I went off into the woodland. I found this view and thought the fallen tree added an interesting slant. I didn't have my DSLR camera with me, so it was down to my camera phone. The clouds started to thin out, and before too long, a magical shaft of light broke through, and illuminated the middle distance. It lasted for about five seconds (or one picture!). It's so true about interesting light making a great landscape picture.

✝ EDDIE POWELL

Glastonbury Festival, Somerset, England

Early evening, near the perimeter fence at Glastonbury 2008 on the last day at 8.04pm. With Leonard Cohen due on stage at 8pm it was a choice between more pictures or missing the master. Cohen won.

✝ JEFF ASCOUGH

Ribble Estuary, Lytham, Lancashire, England

This image was taken in March along the Ribble estuary. Lytham is famous for its shrimping, and the fishermen's boats litter the coastline at this time of year. I was drawn to the isolation of this one boat and the footprints in the mud, and to the beautiful light breaking through the clouds.

PHONE VIEW
youth class

PHONE VIEW YOUTH CLASS WINNER

JAMES BAMBRIDGE ⋯⟩

Tideswell, Derbyshire, England

I took this photo while mountain biking on the farm lanes that surround the village of Tideswell in the Peak District National Park, Derbyshire. It was taken late one evening in April. It took a while to get everyone to look at the camera, but we pretty much got there in the end!

ALISHIA FARNAN ⋯⟩

Bridge over railway line, Motherwell, Scotland

I was walking to meet my brother when I noticed that the bridge was ideal for a photograph. Before then, I hadn't taken much notice of it as it was just the bridge I crossed to get over the railway, now I saw it as a prime example of an urban landscape.

MARK BAUER (p.3)
Pentax 67 mark II, 45mm lens, 2-stop ND grad filter, tripod, Fuji Velvia 50. Image scanned to be as close to the original transparency as possible.

MICHAEL DUDLEY (p.5)
Nikon D70, DX Nikkor 12-24mm zoom lens at 18mm and using aperture priority exposure mode. The image has been digitally manipulated.

MIKE CURRY (p.13)
Olympus E1 (modified to take infra red images only), 14-54 2.8-3.5 lens at 14mm. 200 ASA, f4, 1/1250 second.

GARY EASTWOOD (pp.16–17)
Canon EOS-5D with 24-105mm f/4 L lens at 24mm. Colour saturation has been boosted slightly and the contrast increased using curves and dodge/burn.

GABRIELLE BARNES (p.19)
Canon EOS 5D, tripod, f22, TV 0.5, ISO 100, 17mm, 0.9 hard grad ND. Levels adjusted on Photoshop Elements.

SIMON BUTTERWORTH (p.22)
Canon 5D. Canon 16-35mm 2.8mmII. Lee.6NDG. A manual blend of two separate exposures. No manipulation. Levels and curves only.

GARY WAIDSON (pp.24–25)
Canon EOS 5D 32mm on an EF 17-40mm f4 L USM. 1/20 second at f4 iso 200. Spotting and contrast management. No filters.

GRAHAM HOBBS (pp.26–27)
Pentax K10D digital camera. Pentax DA 50-200mm zoom lens at 88mm (35mm equivalent: 132mm); ISO 100, 0.7s at f/16. Tripod mounted. Original image PEF raw file, sRGB colour space. Converted to TIFF (Pentax Photo Lab), Adobe 1998 RGB (Photoshop 5). No digital manipulation or enhancement undertaken at any stage.

PAUL HOLLOWAY (p.28)
Canon 5D, 17-40 f4 lens, Exposure f22, 0.5 seconds. Two-stop ND grad filter.

MARK BAUER (p.29)
Canon EOS 1Ds Mk II, Canon 17-40mm lens, two stop ND grad filter, tripod. Shot in raw and processed in Adobe Lightroom, with levels, curves and white balance adjustments.

FAN FU (pp.30–31)
Canon EOS 30D Sigma 70-200mm f2.8 Lens f/11 1/320 second. ISO 100 Image was digitally manipulated from colour to monochrome in Photoshop CS2. Used levels, dodge and burn, and sharpening.

MARK TIERNEY (p.32)
Canon EOS 5D, with 17-40 lens set at 17mm and ND grad filter. ISO 100. Raw setting and tripod. This is an HDR image with three exposures, one stop apart, tone-mapped in post-production. There has been a curve adjustment and some sharpening.

ADAM BURTON (p.33)
Canon EOS 5D, Canon 17-40L.

GIOVANNI RUSSELLO (p.34)
Canon EOS 5d, with 17-40mm lens set at 17mm 20 second exposure at f/16, using mirror lock-up (MLU), tripod, and remote control. Basic digital workflow on raw and final TIFF image (curves and selected saturation to get a 'Velvia' look).

IAN CAMERON (p.35)
Pentax 67II, 55-100 zoom, polariser, 0.6ND soft grad, f/22 at 1/4 second, Velvia 50. (spot metered from sunlit green slope). Unaltered.

VERENA POPP-HACKNER (p.36)
Toyo Field 45 AII (large format film camera).

MIKE SHARPLES (p.37)
Nikon D2X with 12-24mm lens. Raw setting and tripod. Aperture of f/22 at 1/125 second. Lee filter gray grad – both 0.6 and 0.9. Photoshop CS2 used for adjusting sky and foreground using curves and for brightness/contract balance.

DUNCAN McMILLAN (pp.38–39)
Taken with Canon EOS 300D and Canon EF-S 10-22mm at 10mm, f4, 30 seconds. Digital manipulation: White balance adjusted to neutralise orange glow from streetlights. Some tonal adjustments to modify contrast and saturation.

STEVE GRAY (p.40)
Olympus E3 with 12-60mm lens. ISO 100, 1/15 second at f/14, unfiltered. The image was converted to monochrome in Adobe Lightroom.

DAVID CLAPP (p.41)
Canon EOS 5D with Contax 28mm lens at f2.

RICHARD OSBOURNE (p.42)
Canon EOS-1Ds MkII with 70-200mm lens at 70mm. 0.9 ND grad filter, 1/640 second at f/9. ISO 200.

PETER RIBBECK (p.43)
Olympus E500 with the 14-45 kit lens. Settings: 14mm at f20 1/30 second. Taken in raw, warmed-up slightly and converted to jpeg using RawShooter.

GAIL JOHNSON (p.44)
Canon 40D 100-400 mm IS lens at 220mm f5.6 1/724. Tripod plus remote shutter trigger ISO 100.

DAVID CLAPP (p.45)
Canon EOS 5D, 70-200mm f/4 lens with 1.4xII extender.

MIKE STEPHENSON (pp.46–47)
Canon EOS 1Ds Mk II with 17-40mm zoom (at 17mm). HDR of five shots ranging in exposure between two seconds and 1/4 second at f16. Merged with Photomatix and slight amount of unsharp mask in Photoshop.

PAUL KNIGHT (p.48)
Canon 1Ds, 20mm lens, ND grad filter, long exposure.

ADAM BURTON (p.49)
Canon EOS 20D, Canon EFS 10-22mm.

NEIL WILLIAMS (p.50)
Canon EOS 10D. Image converted to B&W and toned in Photoshop. Edges darkened a little and film grain added.

RICHARD JOHNSON (p.51)
Digital SLR camera – Canon EOS 1Ds Mark III. Single exposure - taken with a small aperture, low ISO setting and moderate shutter speed. Contrast was adjusted by use of curves applied selectively, using the normal blending mode and finally, sharpening was added.

WALTER LEWIS (p.52)
Nikon D70 f14 1/400 second ISO200.

JOE BOWES (p.53)
Canon EOS 5D with 70-200mm lens. Two second exposure at f/18. Filters – 0.6 ND grad, Red 25. Selenium toned in Lightroom.

GARY McPARLAND (p.54)
Canon EOS 5D with Canon 17-40mm lens. 0.8 sec at f/22, ISO 50. Raw setting, processed in Photoshop.

BAXTER BRADFORD (p.55)
Ebony SU45 with Schneider 110mm Super-Symmar XL lens with staggered Lee ND grad filters, Fuji Velvia 50 film. Exposure was one minute.

MIKE BREHAUT (p.56)
Canon 5D 17-40L. Shutter speed 1/15 second at f/9 ISO 50. Second exposure of 1/40 taken for the sky as graduated filters would have destroyed the detail in the far right cliffs.

IAN CAMERON (p.57)
Pentax 67II, 55-100 zoom, polariser, 0.6ND grad, f/16 at one second, Velvia 50. Unaltered.

KATE BARCLAY (pp.58–59)
Nikon D200, Sigma 10-20mm lens f/16 at .8 second ISO 100. Exposure mode – manual flash used.

ALAN YOUNG (p.60)
Canon EOS 5D with 17-40mm USM lens. ISO 100. Exposure 1/125 second at f/9. Edited in Photoshop CS3 and HDR technique used.

IAN CAMERON (p.61)
Contax ST, 80-200 zoom, polariser, 0.45 ND grad, f/22 at ½ second, Velvia 50. (Spot metered from the green strip of illuminated grass). Unaltered.

ADAM SALWANOWICZ (p.62)
Canon 1DS MKII, 24-105mm, at 24mm, f/13, ISO50. 10 Vertical shots +2,0,-2 each for HDR. Photomatix was used for HDR. PTGui was used for panorama stitching.

ADRIAN BICKER (p.63)
Mamiya 645 Pro with 55-110mm f/4.5 lens and polariser on Fuji Velvia. Scanned with an Epson V750 PRO controlled by SilverFast. Removal of dust specks and film grain from sky only.

IAN CAMERON (p.64)
Pentax 67II, 55-100 zoom, polariser, 0.45 ND grad, f/16 at 1/4 second, Velvia 50. Unaltered.

STEVEN WESTLAND (p.65)
Canon 5D, 28-300mm lens at 70mm. Digitally enhanced contrast and removal of a few dust spots.

STEVE BARKER (p.66)
Canon EOS 30 Sigma 28-300mm. Kodak Elite Chrome Extra Colour film.

PAUL KNIGHT (p.67)
Canon 1Ds, 28mm lens.

MIKE BONSALL (pp.68–69)
Canon EOS 5D with 17-40mm lens at 2mm. 10 second exposure at f/22. ISO 100. Lee three-stop hard grad filter.

NEIL MacGREGOR (p.70)
Olympus E3 with 14-54 Zuiko Lens. one second at f22. 100 ASA Cokin ND + ND medium grad. Levels adjustment in Photoshop.

JON TAINTON (p.71)
Canon EOS 5D. Aperture F32, ISO 100, Shutter Speed 1/25 second, focal length 131mm. Manual focus, mirror lock up and tripod. The Image has been digitally manipulated in Photoshop CS2 for colour and luminosity.

DAVID J WHITE (p.72)
Nikon D200, Sigma 10-20mm Lens at 14mm, 1/180 at f8. The same raw file was converted twice, once for the sky, once for the land, and then combined.

GRAHAM McKENZIE-SMITH (p.73)
Nikon D200 Lens : Sigma 10-20mm ISO: 100 Exposure: 1/250 at f8.0. The image is actually two exposures manually blended together (no blending software) using Photoshop CS. Nothing has been added or removed to enhance the composition.

MIKE BREHAUT (p.74)
Canon EOS 5D 17-40L, shutter speed one minute at f/11. Two ND grad filters used, a .6 and .9 to balance the long exposure.

WAYNE SHIPLEY (p.75)
Canon EOS 30D. 1/160 second at f/7.1. ISO 100. Focal length of 18mm. Digitally manipulated in Photoshop CS3.

PAUL CORICA (p.76)
Canon 400D; Sigma 10-20mm set to 10mm; four second exposure; f22.

ROSS ARMSTRONG (p.77)
Canon EOS 20D, Canon EF-S 10-22mm wide-angle zoom lens. Shutter Speed: 1/25 second, Aperture: f/5.6, ISO: 100. Focal length: 10mm (35mm equivalent – 16mm). Centre-weighted average metering, Hoya Super HMC Pro1 77mm polarising filter Cokin P 121 G2 ND8. Grey ND grad filter. Tripod. Image converted from raw. Curves adjusted and image sharpened in post-processing.

MALCOLM BLENKEY (p.78)
Canon 400D 55mm f 5.6 1/60 second. Tripod. Minor manipulation of levels and unsharp mask.

PETER RIBBECK (p.79)
Olympus E500 with 14-45mm kit lens set at 26mm. 1/80 second at f/13. Cokin p121 grad used to balance sky. Converted to jpeg using RawShooter. Slight curves and sharpening applied in Corel Paintshop Pro.

JASON THEAKER (p.80)
Canon 350D bracketed on a tripod at f22. The shot was then edited to gain the biggest dynamic range, as my ND grads wouldn't have retained the detail in the upper rocks. I also removed dust spots, did the mono conversion, curves, levels and noise reduction in Photoshop. I try to keep postproduction to an appropriate level to maintain congruence with the scene represented.

PHILIP SEARLE (p.81)
Canon EOS 1D MK II with Canon 17-14mm F4L lens set at 17mm. 10 second exposure at f22, ISO 50 with 2 x 0.6 Lee ND grad filters. Final image tone mapped and then levels, curves adjusted in Photoshop.

SIMON BERRY (p.82)
Nikon D300 18mm-200mm Nikon Lens f3.5 Shutter speed 1/2000 Aperture Priority. Slight adjustment using levels in Photoshop.

RICHARD EDWARDS (p.83)
Canon 5D (ISO 50) with a 24mm-105mm (at 100 mm) lens and using a .4 ND grad Lee filter. The camera was attached to a Manfrotto tripod with panoramic head. This is an HDR image created using bracketed exposures. The individual HDR files were made using Photomatix Pro, assembled on my Mac Pro using PTGui Pro, and the resulting HDR panoramic image was then tone mapped in Photomatix Pro. I then removed the dust bunnies and odd digital artefact in Photoshop, and applied a small amount of un-sharpen mask.

DAV THOMAS (p.84)
Nikon D200 with Tamron 12-24mm lens (at 12mm). Three stop hard graduated filter and Polariser. Tripod and wellies. I used a three second exposure to provide the movement in the seaweed, giving a sense of the slowly incoming tide. Levels, curves and some saturation increase in Photoshop.

PETER BIRCH (p.85)
Fuji S2, Nikon 18-70mm set at 37mm. Shot composed of a 3-way bracket (one stop apart) merged in Photoshop and curves added.

RON WALSH (p.86)
Canon EOS 5D, Lens EF 24-70mm, Focal length 32mm, Exposure 1/8 second at f /14. ISO 50, Canon raw file, Manual exposure. Imported as a DNG file into Lightroom. In Lightroom; Exposure + 0.25 Increased clarity, vibrance and added saturation Tone Curve; Lights +20 Darks −21 Saturation: Blue +6 Imported onto CS2 Removed dust spots from the sky, added 81K warm up filter, adjusted levels for the sky, applied unsharp mask, flattened image, saved as 8 bit TIFF.

TIM PARKIN (p.87)
Canon EOS 5D Canon 24-105 f/4 at 24mm Exposure – 30 seconds at f/11. Digital Manipulation: three shots across, two exposures. Merged and blended in Photoshop.

MATT KEAL (p.88)
Canon EoS 20D f8 1/160 75mm lens raw format.

REBECCA CUSWORTH (p.89)
Canon 350D, 18-55mm kit lens, Cokin ND grad, 1/250 second, f/10.0, levels adjusted and yellow hues subdued in Photoshop.

ANATOLE SLOAN (p.92)
Nikon D300, 18-200mm lens. Colours were individually adjusted, and some areas were digitally manipulated (dodge and burn).

SERGE MOSESOV (p.93)
Nikon D40X with the 18-55 kit lens. The photo was created from merging three different exposures to make up the final HDR image.

LIAM LESLIE (p.94)
Nikon D200, Nikkor 18-70mm lens. Image digitally manipulated, Infrared filter over lens.

ELOISE ADLER (p.95)
Nikon D50 with 18-55mm lens at 18mm. Sky: 1/6 second at f/22. Pools: 1/2 second at f/22. Foreground: 3 seconds at f/22. The three exposures were combined using Photomatix software.

JASON INGRAM (p.98)
Nikon D2X Lens: 17-55mm F2.8 Settings: 1/8 second at f8. Filters: ND grad 0.6 (two stops).

KEVIN WALSH (pp.100–101)
Nikon D2X. 15 second exposure at f/2.5 ISO 200. Image not manipulated.

DAVID DAGGAR (p.102)
The image was captured on Fuji Provia 100F using a Hasselblad 503cw with a 160mm lens. I scanned the transparency and then carried out minimal digital manipulation with Photoshop.

ANDREW MIDGLEY (p.103)
Fuji TX1 camera + 45mm lens, Fuji Velvia.

ALEX WOLFE-WARMAN (p.104)
Nikon FE2 with Fuji Neopan 400 35mm film. Nikon 135mm lens. I have slightly lightened and sharpened the image in Photoshop and made sure the causeway is absolutely parallel.

STEPHEN EMERSON (p.105)
Canon EOS 400D with Canon EF100-400mm IS lens set at 160mm. 1/320 second at f/9. ISO 200. Tripod.

IAN McDONALD (p.106)
Canon 1Ds MkII, lens EF24-105mm at 105mm, ISO 400, 1/320 at f7.1.

ANDY McGREGOR (p.107)
Panasonic Lumix DMC FZ-18 f5.6. Straightening, noise reduction and sharpening in Photoshop.

DAVID BROOKER (p.108)
Canon 300D with Canon 70-210 lens at 200mm. ISO 100, 1/1000 second at f5.6.

JOHN MARTIN (p.109)
Nikon D300 with Sigma 10-20mm lens. Image taken at 10mm end, shot as raw file, converted to TIFF. Manual exposure, ISO100 equivalent; f11, 1/160 second exposure.

RICHARD BURDON (p.110)
Nikon D200 with 10-20mm lens at 10mm. (35mm equivalent 15mm). ISO 100. 1/160 second at f/8. Digital adjustments – HDR, levels, curves, sharpening, crop.

PETER SPECK (p.111)
Canon EOS 10D; 17-40mm lens at 17mm f8; 1/180 second; ISO 100; Curves adjustment to restore contrast.

PETER STEVENS (p.112)
Nikon D200, 18-70mm lens at 52mm. ISO 100. 1/50 second at f/9. Raw setting.

ANDREW JONES (p.113)
Canon EOS 30, Canon EF20-35mm lens, Tripod, Fuji Velia 50, Scanned from slide (Nikon Coolscan V ED), digital changes to brightness and saturation. Sharpening applied.

ALEX WALLACE (p.114)
Canon EOS 1 DS MkIII, 16-35 f/2.8 L USM II lens. Lee, 0.9 ND grad filter, 1/80 second, f/5.6.

JONNY THOMPSON (p.115)
The image was taken with a Fuji 6x17 Panoramic Camera on Agfa RSX 100 film. It was then scanned on an Epson Perception 2450. The only digital manipulation was some tweaking in the scan's levels, and then dust and scratch removing from the large piece of film.

ANDREW TOBIN (p.116)
Canon 1D Mark III, ISO400, f/18, 1/125 second, 65mm. Image converted to monochrome using Photoshop.

SIMON KENNEDY (p.117)
Canon EOS 5D, Olympus Zuiko 24mm f2.8, High ISO for some noise/grain. Two exposures blended in Photoshop, toning and contrast adjustment in Photoshop, some dodging and burning.

PHIL JONES (p.118)
Canon 40D, Sigma 18-200 OS lens at 18mm, f6.3, 1/60 second, polarising filter and tripod. Original image in raw, processed in Lightroom and Photoshop CS2.

GRAHAM SMITH (p.119)
Canon EOS 5D, 50mm lens.

CHRIS FRIEL (pp.120–121)
Canon EOS 40D In camera – black and white jpeg.

DAVID BAKER (p.122)
Canon EOS 5D, EFS17-40mm f4 L USM, 1/160 second at f11.

BEN EVANS (p.123)
Shot with a Nikon D70s and Nikkor 18-70mm lens at f/3.5. Crop, contrast increase, desaturation and vignette in Photoshop.

GEOFFREY LAUDER (pp.124–125)
Nikon D70s with Tamron AF 28-300 zoom lens and Hoya polarising filter.

PAUL TURNER (p.126)
Canon Digital Ixus 400 compact camera, 4 Mega Pixels. The image was captured on manual mode and hand held. A little Photoshop work has been carried out to enhance and balance the sky tones and to increase lightness and contrast in the foreground.

BILL ALLSOPP (p.127)
Canon EOS 5D; 24-70 mm lens at 24mm 1/250 second at f8; ISO 400. I do not use filters, preferring instead to bracket, or as on this occasion, process the raw file twice, once for highlights and once for shadows, then blend. This gives me more control over the finished image.

COLIN CADLE (p.128)
Nikon D2X, 1/500 second, f/11, 17-55mm f/2.8 lens set at 31mm, handheld, slight adjustment to levels in Adobe Lightroom.

RICHARD HARRIS (p.129)
Canon EOS 350D with 28-80mm lens. 1/2000 second at f/20 using ISO 1600 to give grainy effect. Contrast adjustment and use of Auto Level tool in Photoshop CS3 and removal of watersplash that had been on lens front.

GARY EASTWOOD (p.130)
Canon EOS-5D with 70-200mm f/2.8 L IS USM lens at 200mm. Colour saturation and contrast levels have been boosted in Photoshop CS3, and the image cropped to 6x17 format.

MARK SADLIER (p.131)
Canon EOS 1Ds MkII with EF 70-200mm IS lens at 180mm. 1/100 second at f/11. Raw file processed in Adobe Lightroom and Photoshop CS3.

ANDREW BARTON (pp.132–133)
Canon EOS 1Ds MkII with 70-200mm IS lens. 1/60 second at f/14. Shot in raw format with slight adjustment to levels, sharpening and cropping in Photoshop.

MALCOLM KAY (p.134)
Pentax K10D, Sigma 18-50 f2.8 EX lens, UV filter. 10 Mp raw image processed with Adobe PS6. 1/350 second, f9.5, ISO 100, AP, 18mm. No digital manipulation.

PAUL SANDY (p.135)
Canon EOS 5D EF 24-105 L IS USM at 105mm ISO 100. 1/400 second at f9.0. Raw file developed in Adobe Lightroom. Slight sharpening applied in Adobe Photoshop.

TERRY FOSTER (p.136)
Nikon D80, Sigma 10-20 lens. Levels, saturation in Photoshop.

GRAHAM McKENZIE-SMITH (p.137)
Camera: Nikon D200 Lens: Sigma 10-20mm ISO: 200 Exposure 1/500 second at f11. I have adusted the levels and used dodge and burn tools on Photoshop CS to help balance the light.

JONATHAN LUCAS (p.138)
Sony DSC F717. 1/350 second at f/6.3. ISO 100.

ANTHONY ANGUS (p.139)
Fuji Finepix F31fd Shutter speed: 1/1500 second. Aperture: f8 Preset on landscape mode.

MAGGIE McCALL (p.140)
Mamiya RZ 67, 180mm lens, tripod mounted, Fuji Velvia 50, rated at 32. f8. Scanned into my computer, the only manipulation involved was to get the digital image to match, as closely as possible, the colour and the clarity of the original transparency.

JULIE CHAMBERLAIN (p.141)
Nikon D80, 18-135mm lens f6.5 1/125 second. ISO 200. Focal length 18mm. Polarising filter Photoshop – Auto contrast.

MIKE DOHERTY (p.142)
Nikon D2X. This image has not been digitally enhanced.

BERNIE BROWN (p.143)
Canon EOS 1D. Focal length of 50mm. 1/60 second at f/16. ISO 400. The flash was fired and the picture was slightly sharpened in Photoshop.

CONNOR MATHESON (pp.146–147)
Canon EOS 400D and Kit Lens.

LAURENZ VOGT (p.148)
Nikon 100.

JESSICA McLAUGHLIN (p.149)
Nikon D40. Focal length of 55mm (35mm equivalent = 82mm). 1/500 second at f/11. ISO 200.

PETE BRIDGWOOD (pp.152–153)
Canon EOS 1Ds Mk II; 70-200mm lens at 70mm 1/250 second. f/11 ISO 100.

HOWARD KINGSNORTH (pp.154–155)
Nikon D2X Lens: 14mm Prime 1/250 second f/2.8. ISO 100.

CHRIS CALVER (p.156)
Canon EOS 5D Canon 17-40 f4L. Exposure 8/10 second. f22 ISO 50. Processed three times. Capture one -1, 0, +1 then combined in Photomatix Pro.

MARI STERLING (p.157)
Canon 5D, Canon 17-40mm L lens, 4 stops of ND grad filter. 0.5 seconds at f/16, ISO 50, manual, evaluative metering, focal length 17mm. Original shot in raw. Contrast, saturation and sharpening tweaks in Adobe Photoshop CS2.

KRIS DUTSON (p.158)
Canon EOS 5D, Canon 100-400 f4.5-5.6 L IS USM, Cokin XPro Grads, Tripod, raw format developed in Lightroom and final levels and curves tweak in PS CS3.

ROBERT McCALLION (p.159)
Fujifilm Finepix S9600, 28-300mm zoom lens, 1/40 second at F5.6, ISO 400, Tripod.

PETER DOBSON (p.160)
Canon 30D; Exposure 1/2500 second. Aperture: f 7.1; ISO 250. The only manipulation to the image has been some cropping to improve the composition, and some exposure and contrast adjustment. The image is presented as a monochrome with a small degree of tint in the shadows colour balance.

ROD LEWIS (p.161)
Canon EOS 5D. Two exposures blended – 1/5 second and 1/4 second 17mm; ISO 100.

KATE BARCLAY (p.162)
Nikon D200, Sigma 10-20mm lens.

CHRIS LOGUE (p.163)
Nikon D40x with 10-20mm lens. 10 exposures merged 1/125th – two seconds at f/16. ISO 100. Dodge and burn and local saturation adjustments applied in Photoshop.

JOHN POTTER (p.164)
Kodak DCS Pro SLR, Canon L series 17-40 lens set at 20mm. F16 1/4 second. ISO 160; B&W Polarising Filter plus Lee ND grad 0.6 filter, Gitzo Explorer tripod.

ROBIN WHALLEY (p.165)
Canon 400D with a Sigma EX10-20mm lens set at 12mm. Correct exposure 1/50 second at f/16, ISO100. This is an HDR image created from three images: one image at -2ev, one image at the correct exposure and one image at +2ev. The camera was tripod mounted.

PAUL KNIGHT (p.166)
Canon EOS 1Ds; 17-40mm lens at 17mm 0.4 seconds; f18; ISO 100.

DAVID BARRETT (p.167)
Pentax K10D, focal length 29mm, exposure one second at f13, a number of exposures were made and blended together to create this final image.

GORDON SCAMMELL (p.168)
Nikon D200; Lens: Nikkor 35mm prime f2.0 1/350 second; f9.0 ISO 200. No manipulation apart from slight adjustment of levels and saturation.

ADAM BURTON (p.169)
Canon EOS 1Ds MkIII, Canon 17-40L.

SIMON KENNEDY (pp.170–171)
Canon EOS 5D, two exposures to capture the dynamic range, blended, toned and contrast-adjusted in Photoshop.

KEITA YASUKAWA (p.172)
Pentax67 camera with a 105mm lens. Fifteen individual negatives scanned in and stitched together.

JONATHAN LUCAS (p.173)
Canon EOS 5D; Sigma 12-24mm lens ISO 200; f6.3; 1/500 second. Shot in raw format and post-processed in Photoshop CS3. I had planned to sepia tone this at the outset along with the square crop that I felt drew the eye towards the birds and perspective of the viaduct better than a wider angle, which would bring in too many distractions. However, I was particularly keen to achieve an authentic 'non-digital' vibe with this, more like the kind of image that would look like it originated from an old film camera. Toning was achieved through many subtle, masked layers of gradient maps, levels and curves.

CHRISTOPHER HARLAND (p.174)
Canon EOS 1Ds MkII. ISO200. 1/600 second at
f11. The image has not been manipulated. Some
sharpening applied and spots removed.

DUNCAN McMILLAN (p.175)
Canon EOS 400D and Canon EF-S 10-22mm at
10mm, f11, 1/80 second. Digital manipulation: A
tone-mapping technique was used to enhance
detail on the underside of the bridge. Some tonal
adjustments to modify contrast and saturation.

RICHARD BURDON (p.176)
Nikon D70 – 10-20 lens at 10mm (35mm
equivalent = 15mm) 200 ISO 1/60 second at
f16. Digital Adjustments: HDR, levels, curves,
sharpening, crop.

LES McLEAN (p.177)
Canon 1Ds MKII Lens: Canon 50mm f1.4. Image
info: 20 seconds at F14, ISO50. Processed with
Photoshop CS3.

MATTHEW JELLINGS (p.178)
Canon EOS 400D 17-85 IS lens Benbo tripod
1/60 second at f20. ISO 100 3 stop ND hard grad
filter. Digital manipulation: Increased saturation,
levels, noise reduction and limited sharpening.

STEEN DOESSING (p.179)
Canon EOS 5D; Schneider-Kreutznach 28mm f2.8
Shift lens. ND 10x filter and Polariser. In addition
to an ND 10x filter, I used a polarising filer.
With the ND filter in place, I had to position the
polarising filter off the camera and then use the
outer ring markings as an alignment point.

MIKE BONSALL (p.180)
Canon EOS 5D with 17-40L lens at 19mm. Lee
Two-stop hard grad filter. 3.2 seconds at f/16.
ISO 50. Raw file processed using Capture One
4. Converted to black and white in Photoshop.
Levels and Curves adjustments plus selective
dodging and burning.

KEITH FOSTER (p.181)
Nikon D2X; 17-55mm at 26mm f5.6 ISO 100 1/125
second. Converted to black and white using
Aperture.

IAN CAMERON (p.182)
Pentax 67II, 200mm lens, f/16 at one second,
Velvia 50. Unaltered.

JOHN PARMINTER (p.183)
Nikon D200, Sigma 17-70mm EX lens at 21mm,
no filters but use of tripod, remote release and
spirit level. ISO 100, 1/3 second, f22 exposure.
Image processed from raw file, dust cleaned,
slight levels/curves contrast adjustment and
sharpening.

JAMES OSMOND (p.184)
Canon EOS 5D. 24-105mm lens. Exposure 4
seconds at f20. Minor curve adjustment.

ADAM SALWANOWICZ (p.185)
Canon DS MKII, 16-36mm, at 17mm, f/16, 1/6
second, ISO50, two stops ND grad. Conversion
to black and white in PS2. PTGui was used for
stitching images.

DUNCAN McMILLAN (p.186)
Taken with Canon EOS 300D and Canon EF
28-135mm at 135mm, f9, 30 seconds. Digital
manipulation: White balance adjusted to
neutralise orange glow from streetlights. Some
tonal adjustments to modify contrast and
saturation.

DAN PRINCE (p.187)
Canon EOS 5D, 24-70mm lens. Colour balanced
and processed in Capture raw.

EMMANUEL COUPE (p.188)
Canon 1Ds, Canon 17-40L lens. Two exposures
masked together in Photoshop.

JANET BURDON (p.189)
Nikon D70 with 10-20 lens set at 11mm (35mm
equivalent = 15mm). 1/250 second at f/5.6. ISO
200. Digital adjustments – HDR, levels, curves,
sharpening, cropping.

ZOË HEMSLEY (p.190)
Canon EOS 300D, Canon 10-22mm lens. 1/80
second at f16, taken at 10mm. Turned to black
in white in Adobe Lightroom. Recovery, fill light
and black sliders used to bring back detail in the
building, and create the grain. Spotted, resized
and sharpened in CS3.

MATTHEW PARKER (p.191)
Nikon D300. I took this shot using the High
Dynamic Range (HDR) technique, hand-held, as
I did not have my tripod with me. HDR software
was then used to give the final image extra
depth. No other post processing was performed.

MATTHEW PARKER (p.192)
Nikon D70 with three exposures then merged
using HDR software. No other post-processing.

ROBIN WHALLEY (p.193)
Canon 400D with Sigma EX10-20mm lens set at
10mm. Correct exposure is 10 seconds at f/11,
ISO100. Tripod. This is an HDR image combining
three images shot at -2ev and +2ev from the
correctly exposed image. The images were
blended and tone mapped using Photomatix
software.

COLIN CAMPBELL (pp.194–195)
Canon 350D; 11-18 mm; f/14; 1/13 second ISO
200; 14mm Levels and saturation in Photoshop
Elements.

SIMON BUTTERWORTH (p.196 left)
Canon EOS 5D. Canon 16-35mm 2.8LII. A manual
blend of two separate exposures (20 seconds
and 71 seconds at f8). No manipulation.

SIMON BUTTERWORTH (p.196 right)
Canon EOS 5D. Canon 24-70mm 2.8L. 10 seconds
at f22. Not manipulated. Levels and curves only.

DUNG HUYNH (p.197)
Canon EOS 5D, Canon 17-40mm lens, Lee ND grad
filters. ISO 100, f16, shutter speed 0.4 seconds.
Colour balance and curves in Photoshop CS3.

KEVIN MARSCH (p.198)
Taken with a Canon EOS 350D. Photoshop to
desaturate, dodge and burn to accentuate
highlights and to bring out detail in the shadows
and noise reduction to add a silky feel to the sky.

FRANK PAYNE (p.199)
Nikon D200 at ISO 100, 1/80 second at f11
with +0.5EV exposure. Lens: 18-200mm set at
48mm. The image has been post processed in
Photoshop CS3.

JOHN FANNING (p.200)
Canon EOS 40D, Sigma EX HSM 10-20mm lens,
f/20 for 5 seconds at 10mm, ISO 200, tripod,
remote release and LEE 0.9 ND grad filter.

LEN GREEN (p.201)
Canon EOS 40D, brightness and contrast
tweaks, digital grad to brighten the foreground,
some dodging on the rocks and pier, in camera
painting with light on the foreground. Nothing
added or removed.

LES FORRESTER (p.202)
Canon EOS 20D with Sigma 10-20 lens and a two
stop grad. f20 at 1/20 second.

ANDREW DUNN (p.203)
Canon EOS 350D with 18-55mm lens at 18mm
with a polarising filter. Exposure 10 seconds
at f/13, ISO 100. Edited for blending between
bracketed exposures and adjusted for contrast
and colour balance.

DAVID ENTRICAN (p.204)
Fuji GX617, 90mm lens, Fuji Velvia RVP film. Lee
0.6 ND grad filter used.

KEITH WASS (p.205)
Fuji FinePix S5600. The image has been
brightened.

JAMIE RUSSELL (p.207)
Pentax *ist DS.

ELOISE ADLER (p.208)
Nikon D50 with 18-55mm lens at 55mm 1/320
second at f5.6. Cropped and lightened a little in
Photoshop Elements.

HARRY TILSLEY (p.209 top)
Panasonic compact DMC-FX8: exposure
1/8 second at f2.8. ISO80. I cropped and
straightened the image to get the final result.

HARRY TILSLEY (p.209 bottom)
Canon EOS 400D with Sigma 18-200 zoom.
Exposure was 20 seconds at f40. I cropped the
image and selected black and white as part of
the editing.

ANDY McGREGOR (p.211)
Nokia N95 Phone f2.8 1/320s Digitally
straightened, cropped and sharpened and a
slight tweak of the levels.

KEVIN LELLAND (p.211)
Sony Ericsson Cyber-Shot camera phone K810i
No manipulation. Transferred from camera to
iPhoto and then exported as a jpeg.

COLIN HOSKINS (p.212 left)
Nokia 6230i Mobile Phone Camera Image
Capture Set To High Resolution 1/30 second
at f2.8 640 ISO. Image digitally manipulated –
levels adjusted slightly.

COLIN HOSKINS (p.212 right)
Nokia 6230i Camera phone. Capture set to high
resolution 1/125 second at f2.8 320 ISO Image
digitally manipulated – colours and contrast
levels slightly adjusted.

EDDIE POWELL (p.213)
Nokia N95. Shutter speed: 1/320 second. f2.8
ISO: 100.

JEFF ASCOUGH (p.213)
Sony Ericsson K700i. The image was converted to
black and white and dodged and burned digitally.
No other manipulation has taken place.

JAMES BAMBRIDGE (p.215)
Apple iPhone with 2MP camera. This photo has
not been digitally manipulated in any way.

ALISHIA FARNAN (p.215)
Sony Ericsson K800i 1/30 second; f2.8 ISO 200.

Bill Allsopp www.billallsopp.co.uk

Anthony Angus www.renderosity.com/mod/gallery/browse.php?user_id=153382

Ross Armstrong www.roscophotographic.com

David Baker www.davidbakerphotography.co.uk

Kate Barclay www.katebarclay.co.uk

David Barrett www.paparazzistyle.co.uk

Mark Bauer www.markbauerphotography.com

Adrian Bicker www.adrianbicker.com

Peter Birch www.peterbirch.co.uk

Malcolm Blenkey www.mblenkeyphotos.co.uk

Mike Bonsall www.mikebonsallphotography.com

Joe Bowes www.bowesimaging.co.uk

Baxter Bradford www.baxterbradford.com

Mike Brehaut www.creativephotography.gg

Pete Bridgwood www.petebridgwood.com

David Brooker www.mappingideas.co.uk

Bernie Brown www.bbphotographic.co.uk

Richard Burdon www.rjbphotographic.co.uk

Janet Burdon www.rjbphotographic.co.uk

Adam Burton www.adam-burton.co.uk

Simon Butterworth simonbutterworth.photography.com

Colin Cadle www.colincadle.co.uk

Chris Calver www.chriscalverphotography.co.uk

Ian Cameron www.transientlight.co.uk

Colin Campbell www.caitlinphotography.webeden.co.uk

David Clapp www.davidclapp.co.uk

Paul Corica www.psimage.co.uk

Emmanuel Coupe www.emmanuelcoupe.com

Mike Curry www.thephotographer.me.uk

Rebecca Cusworth www.rebeccacusworth.com

Peter Dobson www.plaurence.co.uk

Steen Doessing www.steendoessing.com

Andrew Dunn www.andrewdunnphoto.com

Kris Dutson www.southernscenicphotography.co.uk

Gary Eastwood www.garyeastwood.co.uk

Richard Edwards www.richardedwardsphotos.co.uk

Stephen Emerson www.captivelandscapes.com

David Entrican www.orange-skies.com

John Fanning www.johnfanning.co.uk

Les Forrester www.faceonimages.co.uk

Chris Friel www.chrisfriel.co.uk

Steve Gray www.stevegrayphotography.com

Len Green www.lengreenphotography.com

Christopher Harland www.artronaut.com

Richard Harris www.richardharris.org.uk

Graham Hobbs www.grahamhobbsphotography.com

Colin Hoskins www.colinhoskins.com

Jason Ingram www.jasoningram.co.uk

Matthew Jellings www.pbase.com/mij99

Gail Johnson www.gailsgallery.co.uk

Richard Johnson www.eophotos.com/?id=70

Andrew Jones www.andrewjonesphotography.com

Matt Keal www.photo-synthesis.co.uk

Simon Kennedy www.simonkennedy.net

Howard Kingsnorth www.howardkingsnorth.com

Paul Knight www.paulknight.org

Kevin Lelland www.lelland.com

Walter Lewis www.spiritoftheland.co.uk

Rod Lewis www.rodlewisphotography.co.uk

Chris Logue www.utopianphotography.com

Jonathan Lucas www.jonathanlucas.com

Kevin Marsch www.kgmarsch.co.uk

Maggie McCall www.maggiemccall.com

Graham McKenzie-Smith www.gmsphotography.com

Les McLean www.lesmclean.co.uk

Duncan McMillan www.duncanmcmillan.co.uk

Gary McParland www.garymcparland.com

Andrew Midgley www.andrewmidgleyphotography.com

Richard Osbourne www.richardosbourne.com

James Osmond www.jamesosmond.co.uk

Matthew Parker www.flickr.com/photos/spondle

Tim Parkin www.timparkin.co.uk

John Parminter www.viewlakeland.com

Verena Popp-Hackner www.popphackner.com

John Potter www.jpotter-landscape-photographer.com

Eddie Powell www.thesculpturepark.com

Dan Prince www.danprince.co.uk

Peter Ribbeck www.flickr.com/photos/85152114@Noo

Giovanni Russello www.grgalleries.com

Mark Sadlier www.marksadlier.com

Adam Salwanowicz www.salwanowicz.com

Paul Sandy paulsandy.co.uk

Philip Searle www.digitalscape.co.uk

Wayne Shipley www.peterhousephotography.co.uk

Graham Smith www.allabouttheimage.co.uk

Mike Stephenson www.captureamoment.co.uk

Mari Sterling www.maristerlingphotography.com

Peter Stevens www.peterstevensphotography.co.uk

Jon Tainton www.8thcolour.co.uk

Jason Theaker jasontheaker.com

Dav Thomas www.peaklandscapes.com

Jonny Thompson www.jonnythompson.co.uk

Mark Tierney www.tierneyphotography.co.uk

Andrew Tobin www.tobinators.com

Paul Turner www.stonecastle-graphics.com

Gary Waidson www.waylandscape.co.uk

Alex Wallace www.alexwallace.co.uk

Ron Walsh www.ronwalshphotography.co.uk

Kevin Walsh www.lemonlightfeatures.com

Robin Whalley www.lenscraft.co.uk

David J White www.davidjwhitephotography.co.uk

Neil Williams www.neilwilliams.co.uk

Alex Wolfe-Warman alexwolfewarman.com

Keita Yasukawa www.keitayasukawa.com

Alan Young www.yungaphotography.com

YOUTH

Eloise Adler www.eloiseadler.co.uk

Gabrielle Barnes www.photosix.co.uk

Alishia Farnan www.flickr.com/photos/alishiafarnan

Liam Leslie www.liamleslie.co.uk

Connor Matheson www.flickr.com/clemphotography

Jessica Mclaughlin www.jessiemac.co.uk

Harry Tilsley web.me.com/harry.tilsley/Home